volume I How to Lead Godly Play Lessons

the complete guide to
Godly Play

Jerome W. Berryman

An imaginative method for presenting scripture stories to children

To Thea,

my beloved
and the cofounder
of Godly Play...

TABLE OF CONTENTS

ACKNOWLEDGMENTS

It is hard to know precisely when or where this book really began. The most likely place and time was probably Bergamo, Italy in the winter between 1971 and '72. I was there, with my wife Thea and our two girls, Alyda, then age five, and Coleen, then age eight (This has been a family affair since the beginning!), studying Montessori education at the Center for Advanced Montessori Studies. My intuition was that the Montessori approach to education would be a good way to facilitate spiritual formation. When Sofia Cavalletti came from Rome to give a lecture for the course in Bergamo, my intuition was confirmed. She had already been at work expanding Montessori religious education with her colleague Gianna Gobbi since 1954. I want to acknowledge Sofia Cavalletti first as a mentor and then as a colleague and friend.

Secondly, I want to acknowledge all the children Thea and I have worked with since we returned to the United States in 1972. They challenged me to move in different directions and to create many—over one hundred!—new lessons and materials beyond those I had learned from my mentor. (When I did this I was being "a good Montessori child," as Sofia called me. I was also following the advice "to follow the child" if I wanted to know children and how their spirituality might be nourished.) Many of the children from the early classes in the 1970s are now married and have children of their own. I have had the honor of being the celebrant at many of their marriages.

This work could not have been developed to its present breadth and depth without the many Godly Play teachers, and especially our national Trainers, who have challenged, laughed, prayed and loved their way into the work (serious play) with children, parents and others who engage in Godly Play. Thank you.

Support for this work also came from Tom Berryman, my brother, who was there almost from the beginning and who now directs Godly Play Resources in Ashland, Kansas. This is where the beautiful and long-lasting Godly Play materials are carefully crafted. Thanks also goes to Sally Seltzer and all the rest of the Godly Players in and near Ashland as well, including another "Jerome Berryman" who works there now.

Many risked much on the new venture of the almost invisible, nonprofit Center for the Theology of Childhood in Houston. I especially want to thank Tom Blackmon and Ann McGinty, who took this risk. Ann was the Center's first Administrator, and Tom is the Director of Program and Development. Chris Hotvedt also labored long and lovingly over the many versions of the lesson manuals, which were the foundation for this publication.

The Center would never have survived its early years without the financial support of many foundations and individuals. I want to thank the Episcopal Church

Foundation, especially Bill Anderson, the Executive Director, and Ann Ditzler for their personal support.

Special thanks also goes to Trinity Grants. Trinity Grants is guided by The Reverend James G. Callaway Jr., Deputy for Grants. The Center for the Theology of Childhood was very fortunate to have Courtney V. Cowart, Th.D. to oversee, challenge and keep us accountable. She helped love this small nonprofit into being. Thanks goes to all at Trinity Wall Street, especially to the Rector, The Reverend Daniel Paul Matthews, D.D., who lead the vast, lovely, complex, faithful and inspirational ministry that takes place there.

The Lilly Endowment has also been very important for the development of the Center and especially this book. Chapter 6 is based on research done in Rome at Cavalletti's Center and at Seattle University in the E. M. Standing archives. In addition, a second grant supported much of the theological research upon which Chapter 7 is based. Thank you, ladies and gentlemen. Those grants came at just the right moment to keep the creative spirit moving.

Likewise, the School of Theology at the University of the South (Sewanee) provided critical support at just the right time. Their many consultations and the great fun we had putting on the two national conferences there during the summer helped this movement grow up and begin to become an organization. My thanks to Dean Guy F. Lytle and the Associate Dean, David C. Moore.

As regards the Programs Center staff at Sewanee I would especially like to express my gratitude to Linda A. Hutton and Edward de Bary. Ed is the Director of the Education for Ministry (EFM) Program, which is a process of theological reflection for adults. He immediately saw the links between the process of Godly Play and the EFM process. (In fact, in Australia some call Godly Play "EFM for children.") David Moore, Linda Hutton and Ed De Bary helped design our training process for adults. Anyone who has ever worked with this wonderful collection of human beings soon realizes that a big reason why they remain so humane is Sarah M. Davis. She coordinates the many activities of the Programs Center. Thanks again Sarah!

There is yet one more institution that I want to acknowledge as instrumental to the continuation and development of this work. It is Christ Church Cathedral in downtown Houston. It is where I served from 1984–1994 as Canon Educator. We continue to feel the support of the Cathedral family. In fact, the Godly Play program we began there back in 1984 continues to flourish. Some of those teachers who began in 1984 still teach. Bruce Atkins, an attorney, is one of those teachers. He has become especially important to their program and the Center, where he serves as a member of our board. In 2002 the Center offices moved to the Cathedral.

Before closing this partial list of contributors to this work, I want to tell a little story about the partnership between myself and this work's publisher. When we we began to get going in earnest with the writing and editing, my beloved Thea was diagnosed with cancer. This and a number of other personal complications had diverted almost all of my energy and attention away from this project. James Creasey, the Publisher, sent the project editor, Dina Strong Gluckstern, to Houston for several days to help get *Volume 1* compiled and moving forward again. It was all here, lying about the office at the Center, but I was unable to do anything with it. There are times when we all need reinforcements and for me this was one of those times. As the project moved along I began to think of "Dina" more as "DNA." Thanks also goes to all the team at Living the Good News and especially to Dirk deVries, who kept the project coordinated and moving smoothly to completion. They have been gracefully competent and great fun to work with.

In the background to all of this are the nourishing comings and goings of family and friends. Our girls, Alyda and Coleen, are now grown and Alyda and Michael Macaluso have three girls of their own. Coleen continues to live with us, to paint and to be a world-class aunt. There is a new dog, Monte, who also deserves my thanks, and I still remember and thank all the critters who came before him, especially Robin and Goat.

INTRODUCTION

Welcome to *The Complete Guide to Godly Play*. In this series of books, I'm not going to make any universal claims, such as "Everyone should do Godly Play, and this is exactly how they should do it." Godly Play isn't something that everyone can or should do. It's just what I do. If I were a painter, I would only tell you how *I* paint. That's not the same as telling you how *you* should paint—or even telling you whether or not you *should* paint.

Learning the power and richness of the Christian tradition's way of communicating is like learning an art. You have to use it to learn it. You will need to practice these lessons, use them with children, reflect on them and do them some more before they will be yours. This is especially important, since all we can really teach the children is how to enter the language to be more fully in God's presence. How can you explain that? You have to show it. Showing it can't be faked. In terms of learning how to do any other art, like painting, you have to pick up the paintbrush, dip it in just the right color, and let your hands move the brush over the canvas.

In *The Complete Guide to Godly Play*, all I want to do is make it clear in print how I do Godly Play and why. I provide many opportunities for you to practice and reflect on this art. If you want to depart from this tradition, that's your choice. But these volumes offer the best description I can give of my own practice so far.

You can travel through this volume, according to your needs. Here is a map of its seven chapters to help you chart your course.

In Chapter 1, I'll explore what I mean by play and describe an adult experience of Godly Play. I'll also explain how I believe teachers, children and churches benefit from a Godly Play program. I'll invite you to reflect on your own experience of Godly Play and what resources you think you might need to support your learning.

In Chapter 2, I'll describe the unique characteristics of *story* as a way of knowing. I'll offer a storytelling exercise that allows you to experience for yourself the process of creating and sharing a story, then describe the different genres of Godly Play presentations. I'll then invite you to reflect on your storytelling experience, and provide questions you can use as you learn several kinds of Christian language as presented by Godly Play. Finally, I'll discuss the importance of story and finish by telling a story about stories.

In Chapter 3, I'll invite you to experience for yourself the qualities of genuine play. We'll explore those qualities in more depth as we discuss why both scientific and theological investigations of play have failed to provide a broad-based definition of play. We'll contrast the qualities of genuine play with the destructive qualities of pseudoplay, and examine four destructive games of pseudoplay found in some religious education. Finally, we'll compare the qualities of genuine play with the Christian language and experience of grace. You will then reflect on your own experiences of play, pseudoplay and grace.

In Chapter 4, I'll introduce you to the pragmatic details of a Godly Play program and discuss how to manage time, space and relationships during a typical Godly Play session. You'll find diagrams that show how to place the materials in the room, a worksheet to help you plan an effective full-year program, a clear guide to the different responsibilities of the two coteachers in a Godly Play session, notes on art materials and suggestions for using Godly Play with older children.

In Chapter 5, I'll introduce ways that Godly Play has been used in settings other than Sunday morning church school. We'll explore how we might encounter children in special situations, such as using Godly Play in pastoral care for hospitalized children. We'll also explore ways to use Godly Play outside at home and in the community. Finally, we'll look at why it matters that we learn to use Godly Play in a variety of settings.

In Chapter 6, I'll tell the story of how I view the Montessori tradition of religious education for children. I'll explore contemporary developments—what I call the fourth generation—of that tradition, including Godly Play and Catechesis of the Good Shepherd. Then we'll look back to trace the history of Montessori religious education from the first generation, featuring the work of Maria Montessori herself, through the second generation, characterized by E. M. Standing, to the third generation, featuring the work of Sofia Cavalletti.

In Chapter 7, we'll explore a theology of childhood intended for adults. I'll explain why we need the perspectives of this theology to come to full maturity ourselves. We'll look at the historical view of children, in theology and in society, then compare and contrast those views with the view Jesus held of children. We'll consider three propositions of a theology of childhood that hold implications for our own maturity *and* for Godly Play.

I hope you'll find what you need here to enter into the most rewarding play of all: *Godly Play*.

CHAPTER 1

WHAT IS GODLY PLAY?

THE WORLD IS A DANGEROUS PLACE

A family in our church suffered the loss of the mother and one son in a car accident. The father, one son and one daughter survived. The surviving son was in my Godly Play class last year. When I told the story of The Great Family, I asked what the most important part of the story was. The boy, then in second grade, said, "The part where you said the desert is a dangerous place is the most important because the world is a dangerous place. Bad things happen like car accidents and people get so mad about it but it just happens."

Another child in the class looked at me and said, "Yeah, his mother and brother were killed in a car accident." Most of the other children seemed to know this already and were nodding their heads. I thought it was so important that the children could attempt to process this tragedy and wonder about it together.

—Cyndy Bishop, Godly Play Trainer

AN INVITATION TO GODLY PLAY

This really is an *invitation* to Godly Play. I can't make you play, because play doesn't work that way. An essential quality of play is its freedom: its lack of compulsion. Do you want to play? Do you want to join in *Godly* Play? If you do, this book can be one way you begin to accept the invitation.

In Chapter 3, I'll explore play in more detail, as well as its counterfeit, pseudoplay, and its divine counterpart, grace. For now, though, I'll begin by describing what I mean by the word *play*. This five-part description, the one I use most often, is based on Catherine Garvey's book *Play*[1]:

1. Play is pleasurable, enjoyable.
2. Play has no extrinsic goals. It is played for itself.
3. Play is spontaneous and voluntary. It is freely chosen by the player.
4. Play involves deep and active engagement on the part of the players.
5. Play has systematic relations to what is not play such as creativity, problem solving, language learning, the development of social roles and a number of other cognitive and social phenomena.

So there really has to be an invitation to play, not a directive based on power or an argument from authority. For you to enter into Godly Play, you must find it enjoyable.

You must want to play it for its own sake. You must choose to play it because *you* want to play that game. You must be willing to let go of the myriad mundane details of daily life and to enter deeply into the timelessness of play.

In Godly Play, the invitation is given not for play in general but for play with the language of God and God's people: our sacred stories, parables, liturgical actions and silences. Through this powerful language, through our wondering, through the community of players gathered together, we hear the deepest invitation of all: an invitation to come play with God.

AN ADULT EXPERIENCE OF GODLY PLAY

To experience Godly Play, you don't need to pretend to be a child. Instead, you can experience for yourself, as a teacher or parent, how a Godly Play session works. If you know of a church with an established Godly Play program, find out if they offer a parent participation session that you might attend. You can also sign up for a teacher accreditation event, offered around the country by experienced Godly Play trainers accredited through the Center for the Theology of Childhood (see Resources, p. 147). For now, though, I'll invite you to join in one adult session we can imagine together right now.

AT THE THRESHHOLD

You approach the door of a Godly Play classroom. Seated by the door is a warm, inviting person—the door person for this Godly Play classroom. Something is already different: you don't walk into this room rummaging through your pockets for a pen or chatting with a neighbor. At this doorway, people stop and get themselves ready to go inside.

The door person smiles at you. "I'm so glad you're here. Are you ready?"

You think for a moment. *Are* you ready? Yes. This is why you've put this time aside—to play. To play with the language of the Christian people. "Yes."

He nods at your answer, and then, because no one is pretending that this is a classroom of children, asks two questions that children don't generally hear at the door of a Godly Play room: "Would you like to sit on a chair or the floor?" and "Do you have a cell phone?"

BUILDING THE CIRCLE

Cell phones turned off, adults make their way into the room. Some sit on chairs. Others sit, as children in a Godly Play classroom sit, in a circle around the storyteller. She is talking quietly and easily with the people in the circle. A Godly Play community begins right here, by building a circle where each and every participant is warmly welcomed.

When everyone is welcomed, the circle is complete. Now the storyteller says, "We need to get ready for the story." She shows how to get ready by sitting quietly, legs crossed, hands at the ankles. The conversation becomes a silence filled with expectation. She smiles and says, "Watch where I go to get this story."

PRESENTING THE LESSON

The storyteller moves to the desert box—a large, shallow, wooden box on wheels, filled with sand. She brings it to the circle. "Keep watching," she says and goes to a shelf filled with beautiful items: a rack of seven wooden cards, an ark with graceful lines, a length of heavy chain. She takes up a basket and brings it to the circle. She opens the lid of the basket and gets herself ready again; now all her attention is on the desert box in front of her. Your own eyes follow her focus and watch the sand.

"The desert is a dangerous place," she says. Her hands slowly move across the surface, smoothing and shifting the sand. "It is always moving, so it is hard to know where you are. There is little water, so you get thirsty and you can die if no water is found. Almost nothing grows there, so there is almost nothing to eat. In the day-time it is hot and the sun scorches your skin. In the night it is cold. When the wind blows, the sand stings when it hits you. People wear many clothes to protect them from the sun and blowing sand. The desert is a dangerous place. People do not go into the desert unless they have to."

She pauses. Then she lays out blue yarn and blocks of wood on the sand. She tells how, after the flood, people went out to the four corners of the earth. They lived along rivers and in villages and in cities. "One city was named Ur." She touches a block. "The people there believed that there were many gods. There was a god for every tree, every rock, every flower. There was a god of the sky, the clouds, the water and the land. The world was alive with gods.

"But there was one family that believed that all of God was in every place. They did not yet know that, but that is what they thought." She places two wooden figures in the sand and names them: *Abram* and *Sarai*, two members of the family who thought that all of God was in every place.

"When it came time to move to a new place, they were not sure that God would be there. So they wondered what the new place would be like." She moves the figures slowly, one at a time, pausing often to keep them together, toward another block. As she moves them, you can see the footprints they leave behind in the sand.

Your eyes focus where her own eyes and hands focus on the small wooden figures moving through the sand. Perhaps you feel a little impatient, wishing she would just pick them up and put them by Haran. Perhaps memories of other times and ways you have heard this story drift into your mind. Perhaps you feel a pang, remembering a journey of your own. Just by growing up, each of us has known what it's like to leave behind a familiar situation for one that is at least partially unknown.

"It took a long, long time," she says. Finally, they arrive at Haran. The storyteller moves the Abram figure away from Haran, into the desert, where he 'came so close to God, and God came so close to him', that Abram knew what they must do: keep traveling. The journey continues, past Haran. They come to Shechem, and Abram prays. God is there. "So Abram built an altar to mark the place." She takes several stones from the basket and makes an altar in the sand.

She moves the figures slowly on. "Abram and Sarai come to Bethel, and God is in this place, too." She takes more stones and builds another altar. "Finally they come to Hebron and make their home. And there God changes their names: they are to be called *Abraham* and *Sarah*. God promises that even though they are old, they will have a baby. Abraham laughs. He and Sarah are too old!"

The storyteller sits back, but keeps her eyes on the figures as she tells how three strangers come and promise again that Abraham and Sarah will have a baby. Abraham and Sarah both laugh, "But do you know what happened?" the storyteller asks, her voice warm with pleasure. "They have a son. They laugh again, so they name the baby *Laughter*, as God told them to do. In their language the word for laughter is *Isaac*."

The storyteller pauses, and then her voice turns more serious as she tells how Sarah died and how Abraham sent his most trusted helper to find a wife for Isaac. "The helper finds Rebekah, 'as full of courage as she was kind'. The helper tells her about Abraham, Sarah and Isaac, and Rebekah travels back to join the great family."

Once more the storyteller moves a figure on the journey, now traveling again over the path made by Abraham and Sarah. She brings the Rebekah figure all the way to where the figures of Abraham and Isaac are waiting. She pauses. "Then Isaac and Rebekah had children, and their children had children, and those children had children. This went on for thousands and thousands of years until your grandmothers and grandfathers had children. Then your mothers and fathers had children."

She scoops up a handful of sand, and lets it trickle out. "Now you are part of that great family which has become as many as the stars in the sky and the grains of sand in the desert." She is so silent that you can almost hear your own heartbeat quicken at the thought of that great family of which you, too, are a part.

WONDERING

The storyteller sits back. Now, at last, she lifts her gaze and looks into the eyes of those seated in the circle as she asks, "I wonder which part of this story you like best?" She draws out the words, her voice careful and inviting. There is a silence almost electric with expectancy. Then one woman answers, "I liked the part where they built altars, because God was in Shechem and Bethel, too."

The storyteller listens, then touches the two stone altars in the desert box. "Altars... because God was in those places, too." Her touch is deliberate, almost reverential.

She looks up again. This time the man sitting next to you speaks. "I like the part where they named the baby *Laughter*." The storyteller grins and touches the Isaac figure. "They laughed again, and named their son *Laughter*," she repeats.

Two other people name their favorite parts of the story, then a comfortable silence settles again. Now the storyteller asks, "I wonder which part of this story is the most important part?"

The first person to answer this question speaks more slowly, as if working out his answer as he talks. "I think...the part about how all of us are now part of the great family, too." The storyteller nods slowly. She lets sand spill from her hand again as she says, "as many as the stars of the sky and the grains of sand in the desert."

Others name the parts where the family finds out that all of God is in every place, or where the family moves to a new home but remains together.

The storyteller affirms each answer and then waits before asking her next question. "I wonder where you are in this story, or what part of this story is about you?"

One woman wrinkles her nose and says, "I think the part where Sarah laughed, because she thought God's promise *couldn't* come true is about me. Sometimes God seems too good to be true!"

There is quiet laughter from several participants, but not a laughter that ridicules the woman. This laughter is a joyful affirmation of her words, the kind of laughter that says, "Yes, I've felt that way, too!" The storyteller touches the figure of Sarah and echoes, "And Sarah laughed."

An older man names the part of the story where Rebekah decides to join the great family as being about him. The storyteller affirms his words as she touches the Rebekah figure.

Finally the storyteller asks, "I wonder if there is any part of this story we could leave out and still have all the story we need?"

People are quiet as they think about this. Perhaps you think of some details you feel are unimportant: the names of the cities from which they came, or the way that God changes the names of *Abram* and *Sarai* to *Abraham* and *Sarah.* Some listeners offer tentative answers. One woman declares that she doesn't think any part of the story can be left out.

The storyteller listens respectfully to *every* answer. She repeats it, touches figures in the sand to illustrate it, but she never calls one answer good or another answer wrong. She simply listens and accepts the responses.

RESPONSE

Finally the wondering sinks into silence. She invites you to watch again as she puts away the lesson, so you'll know where to find it. She asks you to think about what work you would like to do in response to the lesson. She shows where there are art supplies waiting.

One woman chooses to work with the desert box, and soon she is seated on the floor, leaning over the box, concentrating on moving the figures for herself. A man says that he wants to paint and walks to where the door person helps him get a tray, a paintbrush, a set of paints and paper. Perhaps you choose to work with crayons. You pick out three colors you want, and put them on a drawing board with a piece of paper.

You find a place in the room to work, and something strikes you about the way people move in silence. You've been in adult classes or groups where as soon as the presenter stopped speaking, listeners began chattering. This is not what happens here. Everyone has been involved in the story and the wondering. Now that absorbed involvement continues as people, one by one, name what response they choose to make and quietly rise to get their materials. For at least a quarter of an hour, people work at their responses. Some people make more than one picture. One person has gotten out a Bible and is reading silently the story of Abraham and Sarah. Another person is writing and making a little book of folded paper.

THE FEAST

The storyteller turns the room lights off: a silent signal to everyone. She waits a moment, until all eyes are on her, and then says, "It's time to put away our work and gather again in the circle. There's no need to hurry. We have all the time we need. When your work is put away, come to the circle, and we'll get ready for our feast." Then she turns the lights back on. You take back your own crayons and drawing board, as others put away paints and story materials. The circle forms again, and the storyteller models getting ready for the feast by sitting cross-legged, hands folded.

One server spreads a napkin in front of you. Another server puts down several crackers, and a third server puts down a cup of juice. The storyteller encourages everyone to wait until everyone has been served, so that prayers can be said before sharing the feast.

The storyteller looks around the circle. "It's such a pleasure to be here with you today. Sometimes being together makes us so happy that we just have to pray. You might want to pray out loud, or to yourself. You might want to pray words you know, or words that come to you. You might not want to pray at all, and that's okay, too. If you say a silent prayer, say 'Amen', at the end, aloud, so we'll know your prayer is done."

She looks to each person in the circle in turn. Some quickly say "Amen." Some pray old favorite table graces, and some simply say words like, "Thank you, God, for this time together." When the storyteller has said her "Amen," you share the feast. Only crackers and juice? No. Something more is here: Community. Gratitude. Presence. God.

SAYING GOODBYE

When the feast is finished, and you have put your trash in the trash basket, the storyteller once more draws the attention of the group. "It's time to say goodbye." One by one people go to the storyteller and she holds out her two hands. Most of these adults take her hands, but some lean forward and hug her. With each person she looks into their eyes, smiles warmly and says a quiet goodbye. "It was a pleasure to have you here today. Thank you for being with us."

REFLECTING:
AN ADULT EXPERIENCE OF GODLY PLAY

If this were a Godly Play children's session, this goodbye would send children out the door to join their parents. In an adult session, though, time would be set aside for the adults to reflect on the experience they shared. You, too, can take some time now to reflect on the experience of reading about this Godly Play adult session:

• Which part of the session did you like best?

....

....

....

....

- Which part of the session is the most important part?

....

....

....

....

....

- Where were you most real in the session? What showed you something special about yourself?

....

....

....

....

....

- Is there any part of the session that could be left out and still leave all the experience we needed?

....

....

....

....

....

GODLY PLAY FOR CHILDREN AND TEACHERS

You still might be wondering: What are the benefits of Godly Play for my teaching? for the children of our church? for the teachers of our church? Godly Play is a distinctive approach to Christian ministry with children, both innovative and deeply grounded in our spiritual tradition:

- Godly Play helps resacralize the everyday things of the world, such as bread, wine, candles, oil, wood, linens and clay. Godly Play reteaches a sacramental worldview in a society that is so often utilitarian and materialistic.
- Godly Play teaches children and adults that being quiet and deliberate about their work can be as satisfying as being noisy, busy and pushy and delivers this counter-cultural message in a comforting and consistent way.

I wonder

- Godly Play provides sensorial materials to work with in a safe, stimulating environment. In this way, Godly Play combines and integrates the two primary gateways to knowing for young children—language (the verbal system) and play (the nonverbal system).

- Godly Play is not a rote or transfer method of teaching and learning. It is a *discovery* method that engages the whole child—hands, heart, mind, senses, intuition. This is the best way for children (and adults!) to internalize what is being taught.

- Godly Play uses craft activities, but uses them differently from most curricula. Rather than have children create something prepackaged, each child creates an expressive response to what is individually thought and felt after receiving the parable or sacred story in a group setting. The children have the opportunity to enter the story, wonder about it and *then* create meaning for their own lives.

- Godly Play respects the many demands placed on teachers' time. Unlike many curricula, in which a teacher must plan new activities and gather new materials every week, a Godly Play classroom maintains a stable setup and routine from week to week. Teachers can focus their attention on entering deeply into that week's story and responding with complete presence to the community of children who gather there.

- Godly Play teaches reliance upon a gracious God who is real and accessible in all the mystery of life, both sad and joyful—rather than dependence upon the transient "magic" that comes from the latest movie, toy or video game.

- Godly Play teaches children to respect the things and people they work with, and to enjoy each with care and patience.

- Godly Play teaches the classic rhythm for living modeled in the Bible: the alternation of action and reflection, engagement and prayer. Godly Play teaches those who teach it and those who learn it to build a spiritual rule (or way) of life.

- Godly Play teaches kindness and mutuality through its rituals and by the way it organizes physical space, objects and the community of children. A Godly Play community embodies the biblical ethic of how people are to live together.

- Godly Play offers a contemporary and child-accessible version of the ancient spiritual practice of *lectio divina*: holy reading, wondering and responding to the Bible's sacred stories. Instead of analyzing God's word, the children meditate in an artistic and kinesthetic way. Godly Play helps children know God and the Bible instead of simply knowing *about* God or *about* the Bible.

- Godly Play teaches that everything in God's creation is charged with the possibility of holiness, including each of us, and that we are in relationship with everything in Creation. There is no sacred versus the profane; all ground is holy ground.

- Godly Play teaches that there is *kairos* time (significant time) as well as *chronos* time (chronological or clock time). *Kairos* time is not concerned with knowing *what time it is*. Instead Godly Play gives us time to see God in the center of daily life and to reflect on what time is for.

REFLECTING: GOING DEEPER INTO GODLY PLAY

If you would like to probe these and other possibilities about Godly Play, you have several resources available to support your journey. This handbook (*Volume 1*) will give you an introduction to Godly Play in a variety of settings, while *Volumes 2-4* will give you the detailed notes you need for each Godly Play presentation. You can also find links to the community of Godly Play teachers and trainers, as well as pertinent theory and research by using the resources in the Appendix (p. 147).

You might want to pause and reflect on where you are in your journey, and how Godly Play can support that journey. Here are some wondering questions about you and Godly Play:

• I wonder what I like best about Godly Play?

....

....

....

....

• I wonder what part of Godly Play could be the most important part?

....

....

....

• I wonder if there is something in my life that especially responds to Godly Play? What is there in Godly Play that is especially for me?

....

....

....

• I wonder if there is any part of Godly Play I could leave out and still have all the Godly Play I need?

....

....

....

....

CHAPTER 2

YOU ARE A STORYTELLER

FIND OUR OWN WAY

One Sunday, when I was teaching my fourth grade class, the story ended and wondering began. After some silence, I looked up at the children and was about to ask another wondering question. As I began to speak, one of the boys said, "Oh no! Here comes another wondering question!"

Another said, "How come you always say, 'I wonder?'"

Before I could say anything, someone said, "That's because she doesn't know the answers either!"

At this point I was not at all part of the conversation as another child said, "No that's not it. She wants us to find our own way."

The circle fell silent. Amazing how the teaching happens without the teacher...

—Nancy St. John, Godly Play Trainer

STORY

Story is one of the most ancient and elemental forms of knowing. In the West, beginning in the 17th century, story as a way of knowing was eclipsed by the technique of knowing that we call science. After the rise of science, story came to be considered inferior or premodern, somehow backward. Stories were fit only for children, the illiterate and the uneducated.

Every epistemological change leaves behind a way of knowing that is less useful than the new view. The idea that stories as a way of knowing must be left behind has been discredited in our time. Our thesis is that story is not a frill, not an ornament, not an illustration, not a diversion, not an entertainment and certainly not backward. Instead, it is a unique way of knowing, as valid as science though entirely different in its usefulness.

Two primary ways of using stories were outlined by Jean LeClerq in his description of the differences between monastic and scholastic uses of scripture in the twelfth century.[2] The monastic approach, known as *lectio divina*, or holy reading, emphasized the act of reading as an act of meditation and prayer. The reader came to the text to seek an intuitive understanding, to grow in wisdom, to savor the aesthetic value of the words and, ultimately, to encounter God. This monastic approach to stories is similar to the way we begin in Godly Play.

The scholastic approach, on the other hand, emphasized the act of reading as an act of questioning and testing. The reader came to the text to seek logical understanding, to grow in knowledge and to analyze the written text for ideas and theories. This process is also of enormous value—but of less relevance if our aim is to grow in relationship with God.

Still, as children approach their teens, this more analytical approach develops in Godly Play, too, to sharpen the children's critical thinking. Too often these analytical skills develop without a deep grounding in the monastic approach, which rests on an appropriation of the oral tradition, known with the body. In Godly Play, we see the integrations and appropriate use of these two ways of knowing in each presentation.

A STORYTELLING EXPERIENCE

At the heart of most Godly Play sessions is the telling of the lesson: a narrative drawn from sacred stories, a parable or the showing of the symbols and actions of a liturgical act. Sometimes this seems daunting to a new teacher of Godly Play, but you already know how to tell stories. Prove this to yourself with this simple exercise.

MAKING AN OBJECT BOX

Make an object box about your own life! (See p. 72 for information on how object boxes are used in Godly Play.) First, get to know the subject of your story: you! Take some notes on these questions:

- What was important to me when I was younger than five? When I was five to ten years old? When I was ten to fifteen years old? Jot down a few notes for each five-year interval until you reach your present age. Don't think you have to list what other people would tell you was most important about that time: that you graduated from school or that you got a job. Think instead about what mattered most to you.
- Circle about six to twelve of these notes, the ones that seem to speak most clearly to you *about* you. Perhaps you learned to play guitar when you were eleven years old, and you still love to spend free time every week just picking out songs on strings. Perhaps you moved to a new place when you were in your twenties, and you never did learn to like it. Again, don't worry about what events others might think should be most important, and don't try to make them all "positive." Pick the events or memories that touch you most deeply.
- Now try to pick objects that symbolize these moments for you, in a full and meaningful way. You can even visit a crafts store that carries miniatures if you feel you

want a tiny guitar to put into your object box. (Instead, you might prefer a special pick or a fragment of sheet music that you love.) Pick one object for each of the stories you want to tell. Put your objects into a beautiful box or basket that also catches the spirit you know to be most holy and real about you.

- You can pick an underlay for your story, too, by picking a color that appeals to you. One person might pick blue because blue reminds him of Jesus' mother Mary and of his own lifelong spiritual longing. Another person might pick blue because blue reminds her of blue sky and blue water and how she has always felt most at home outdoors. Find a cloth in the color you choose that is long enough to hold, in order, each of the objects you choose. Roll up the cloth and put it with your box or basket.

TELLING YOUR STORY

Now you are ready to tell your story, either to yourself or someone else. Roll out the underlay for a few inches, enjoying the color you have chosen to tell this story. Place the first object onto your underlay and tell about the story that object represents. Take your time. Listen to your own story, even if you are telling it to someone else. Continue with each of the objects, unrolling the scroll of your life as you go, until you have told your story.

REFLECTING: A STORYTELLING EXPERIENCE

- What did you select? What did you leave out?

....

....

....

....

....

- Why would it be important that *you* be the teller of this story?

....

....

....

....

....

- How would you describe the things you picked out as important? Can you name any themes that link or connect the objects you selected?

....

....

....

....

- How do you tell your story differently from the way that somebody else in your life might tell your story, for example, a parent, partner, child or long-standing friend?

....

....

....

....

....

GODLY PLAY STORIES

THE GODLY PLAY PROCESS

When you have made, told and reflected upon an object-box story of your life, you have experienced the process underlying a Godly Play lesson. Did you tell *every* event of your life? No. That would take as long as the living of it. When I tell a Godly Play story, I carefully choose which details of the story I will share. In telling The Ten Best Ways to Live (*The Complete Guide to Godly Play, Volume 2*), the story of the Ten Commandments, I don't focus on the incident with the golden calf. The heart of the story of the Ten Commandments is what I want to communicate: God helped God's People by giving them The Ten Best Ways to Live.

Did you need to use notes? No. The objects themselves brought to mind the events of your life that you wanted to share. When I tell a Godly Play story, I don't read the story, and I don't even memorize it. I *tell* it, from my heart. I enter into the story with all the presence and attention I can bring, knowing that each time I tell this story I will discover something new. As you might tell the story of your own life differently each time, so we do the same with God's stories. Our different life experiences, our different developmental stages and different personalities mean that each of us will tell Godly Play stories in a unique way.

Did you surprise even yourself with the connections you found in your objects? When I tell a Godly Play story, I open my ears, not just my mouth. I listen for the connections and themes that come alive when I share the stories of the People of God. Over the years, many phrases have found their ways into many Godly Play stories:

- The desert is a dangerous place.
- They were on the same journey we are.
- There was once someone who said such wonderful things and did such amazing things that people followed him.

We experience these connections and themes in many ways, but perhaps with special force in three themes around which I organize Godly Play presentations: sacred stories, parables and liturgical actions.

SACRED STORIES

Sacred stories stimulate our sense of Christian *unity,* while at the same time providing raw materials for the development of a coherent, mature sense of Christian *identity.* In sacred stories, we tell the story of God's People to invite children to become, themselves, part of that story. The story of God and God's People is almost the story of a favorite game of child's play: Hide-and-Seek. God calls people into relationship, who then respond by trying to connect with what they experience as an Elusive Presence. Both words of the phrase are significant: we cannot fully capture our experience of God in any story or rite—yet it is God's presence that invites us endlessly to follow what glimpses we find. The very existence of the game communicates to us the existence of a divine Player. This game is played for the pleasure of its playing and not to win or lose, which would end the game. As we seek and find, we could sum up our story with the word *Aha!* Another glimpse!

Godly Play sacred stories move from the story of Creation to stories of Jesus and the Church. One synthesis lesson for the sacred stories is the story of the Books of the Bible (*The Complete Guide to Godly Play, Volume 2*). The primary synthesis lesson is the story of the Trinity (*The Complete Guide to Godly Play, Volume 4*).

PARABLES

Parables stimulate our sense of *creativity*. In parables, we enter with wonder to live the question. Parables question our everyday view of life. They wake us up to see in life what we have not seen before. Parables question the status quo, the order imposed by tradition, power or class. That is why Jesus' parables often got him into trouble, and why Christians ever since have sometimes redefined parables in ways that only comfort us rather than challenge us by disrupting our comfortable world views. We can sum up the startling quality of parables with a laugh: "Ha ha!" Jesus' parables can make us laugh aloud as they turn our accepted worldviews upside down.

Godly Play parables include six guiding parables as well as parables *about* parables. The parable stories for older children also include parable cards, "I Am" cards and parable games that invite children to play more deeply with the language of these valuable lessons.

LITURGICAL ACTIONS

Liturgical actions stimulate our sense of *integration* of identity (given through sacred stories), of the creative process (given through parables), and of the unspoken presence of God (given through silence). In liturgical actions, we mark life, time and space, so children can know the Holy. As in the great liturgical actions of the whole Church, Godly Play liturgical actions evoke a wholehearted aesthetic appreciation of "Ahh..."

Godly Play lessons are not the liturgy itself. Neither are Godly Play lessons simply talking *about* the liturgy. That kind of scholarly approach would not invite children to enter deeply into the offered experience. Instead, Godly Play liturgical actions present a kind of language lesson. Children can learn the language of liturgy and have an appropriate place to practice the language of liturgy, so that they can enter more fully into the liturgical experience of their own church.

Liturgical action lessons are the lessons that most especially need adaptation to the practice of your own church. The lessons chosen and the symbols used to communicate those acts of worship need to reflect the actual practice of your church. For example, many churches use three purple candles and one rose candle in an Advent wreath. If your church uses four purple or blue candles, you want the materials you use to reflect that.

PRACTICE

Choose one or two stories at a time from each of the three presentation genres: sacred stories, parables and liturgical actions. Learn to tell the stories, either on your own or working with others.

An especially useful way to practice these stories is to work in triads, the practice method used in Godly Play teacher accreditation events. In this kind of triad, one person takes the role of storyteller, one person takes the role of listener and a third person takes the role of observer. The storyteller directs his or her focus on the story (during the presentation) and then to the listener (during the wondering). The listener enters as fully as possible into experiencing the story as a listener. Only the observer keeps the story script handy and watches both storyteller and listener, making notes in order to give constructive feedback at the end of the presentation. At the end of the practice, the observer can first use the questions below to help the storyteller reflect on his or her experience. Then both observer and listener can offer feedback that emphasizes what they appreciated most in the storyteller's presentation.

REFLECTING: GODLY PLAY PRESENTATIONS

Whether working on your own or with others use these questions to reflect on your experience:

• Where did you find yourself in the story? What part of the story was about you?

• What was difficult for you in the story?

• What might you say or do differently the next time you tell this story?

• What did you wonder about?

• How was this presentation different from the presentation of a sacred story (or a parable or a liturgical action)?

- How was the wondering that followed this presentation different from the wondering after a sacred story (or a parable or a liturgical action)?

....

....

....

....

- What did you see or hear or experience that will help you the next time you present a sacred story (or a parable or a liturgical action)?

....

....

....

....

- What more would you like to know about presenting a sacred story (or a parable or a liturgical action)?

....

....

....

....

THE IMPORTANCE OF STORIES

Children love to hear and tell stories, a natural medium of childhood communication. (Another natural medium of communication is play, the subject of Chapter 3.) Stories are where all of us, children and adults together, find our identity, our family. Stories are where we challenge the deadly messages of the powers-that-be, whether greed and overwork or poverty and powerlessness, that would rob our lives of relationships and meaning. Stories are where we integrate the experiences of our life into powerful acts of recognition, celebration and meaning as we make our way through time and space.

Through story we invite one another to make meaning of our world and ultimately of our lives. In research done in Houston, one common factor found in at-risk youth was that they had no stories. Sharing stories and fully entering into the stories we share is also one way we learn to be genuinely mature. If an adult can't play, or can't enter into Godly Play, that adult cannot invite children into play, either.

But to carry stories within us is to become wisdom-bearers, *God*-bearers, like Mary herself. The elders of a community tell their stories, and children find meaning in those stories and relationships with those elders. Perhaps the best way to sum up many of the possibilities and limitations of narratives and language itself is to tell a story. Listen...

STALKING THE WILD STORY

Once Upon a Time......
Long Ago and Far Away...
There Was Once a...
In the Village of...
When your Mother Was a Little Girl...
A Certain Man...
In the Spring, When Kings Go Forth To War...
Midway in the Journey of Life...
It Was the Best of Times and the Worst of Times...
In the Beginning...

We checked our equipment again at the edge of the territory. It was clear that our hunting gear was too cumbersome. It was for catching domesticated stories. This hunt was for a wild one.

We carefully placed our literary microscopes in an extra tent. It would protect what we decided not to take. Definitions were also placed there. They were too narrow. Every explanation was then pulled from our packs and left behind. They might become stories over time, but only about explaining stories and making rules, not about the wild and unruly.

"Do we need these cases of Freud?" someone asked. They show how stories hide stories, but can repressed stories be wild? Doubt about doubting stories caused us to remove the cases along with several boxes of jargon. Such word traps would only generalize and miss any wildness we might find.

The pile of discarded hunting gear grew. Old saws, noun knives, syllable scissors and other instruments for making sharp distinctions were added. We wanted a living story—not one cut into pieces like the "real author," "the implied author," "the explicit commentary," "the implicit commentary," "the real reader," "the implied reader," etc.

Getting rid of our extraneous equipment refreshed our spirits, but after a moment worry reappeared. We stood there—looking at our descriptions, explanations, cases, jargon, analysis and other equipment lying on the canvas floor of the tent by the fire. It was all so accepted, so normal. The audacity of our hunt had begun to sink in.

Still, the plan to travel light was a good one. We could quickly follow any eaves-droppings we found to the end and then wait in ambush. The only trouble was that no one had ever seen the spoor of a wild story. It didn't help to know that one of the greatest hunters of all time wrote:

A word is dead
When it is said,
Some say.
I say it just
Begins to live
That day.[3]

How can you catch a story that doesn't begin until it ends? Despite these questions we finished lightening our packs and pulled them on.

A final review of the maps confirmed our route. The starting points discovered down a rabbit hole and through a looking glass were bypassed. The wardrobe, where way in the back stories had been found, was again overruled. The classical "*Una silva oscura*," the dark wood Dante entered, which was so clearly marked on the old leather map, was likewise excluded.

We reaffirmed our decision to not toil up the steep path to the abbey, dominated by the uneasy *Aedificium*, the huge maze of a library. We remembered how its silent "testimony to truth and to error," was reduced to ashes. No doubt there were still stories lurking in the blackened ruins, but we would not begin there either. We would neither go beneath the waves or through smoke to hunt. We discussed again Middle-Earth, a place peopled with hobbits and talking foxes, but also rejected it.

We would go to the West End of the nave at Chartres. It was there the great laby-rinth had been laid into the cathedral floor. This had been done sometime between the Great Fire of 1194 and 1220, when the Fulbert section was completed. Everyone nodded in agreement once again, so we broke camp.

After slowly spiraling into the center of the stone labyrinth, we gathered in the six-petaled rose, some nine feet across. It provided us with a damaged doorway. The copper, brass and lead pieces of the original center were gone, removed by Napo-leon's troops. This was a critical moment. One legend said that a Minotaur lurked in the middle, but our fear was overcome by the lure of the hunt. We stepped through to the other side.

On the other side was a forest, but it was neither dark nor wild. It was only strange, yet not too strange, like when an American travels in Australia or an Australian travels in America.

Game trails crisscrossed the gray grass beneath the trees. The path we followed was marked by a faint spray of symbols on several tree trunks and an occasional pile of words in the grass. It led us deep into the thickening forest. As it grew darker we soon became aware of little bursts of light all around us.

"What's that?"

"Lettering bugs. I've only seen them a few times before. They blink at random but are a bit more independent than the spoor we've been following. A story could be stirring them up."

When we stepped into the sunshine of a small clearing another surprise awaited us. Little, black lines came inching toward us from the fringe of the forest all around us.

"What are those things?" another hunter asked.

"I think they are word worms. Do you see how they sometimes couple into longer segments like sentences? I don't think they are dangerous. They also show a story may be near."

Suddenly the forest about us exploded with a great flock of birds swooping up from the trees. They wheeled above us and then dove straight at us with raucous cries, their wings slicing the air.

"Verb birds! Watch out!"

We ducked under fallen trees and behind rocks. The word worms became extremely animated as the birds swooped in. Some attached themselves to the birds and were lifted aloft. A few dug themselves into the ground. Most wove themselves together to trap the birds in their net. The meadow was as animated as a telephone book with the word *begat* inserted between the names!

"Stay down. Traces of stories are everywhere."

Time drifted. We grew bored. Then, as the silence deepened, we heard breathing coming from the trees.

"It has been stalking us," the hunter next to me whispered.

The clipped breathing jerked quickly and invisibly around us in the forest. It sounded like a clock. Every "tick" implied a "tock." Where was it going?

"Look! There it is!" a hunter near the trees shouted.

A vague shape hovered for a moment in the shadows.

"It's got a beginning, middle and end," another hunter shouted.

We looked where he pointed, but the creature had completely vanished.

"How could you do that?" We moved toward the one still pointing. "That definition you threw scared it away."

"I thought we agreed to leave them behind," another hunter harshly whispered.

"I'm sorry. It really only had a beginning and a middle anyway. I know which way it went. I'll show you."

"No. Let's wait. It still seems curious. It was following us, gathering itself, until we startled it. Perhaps, it will come back if we remain quiet."

Another hunter said, "I think it's too scared to do that, but we might be able to get it to come back and play."

"How do you do that?"

"Well, we can't force it to play. I know that. We can only invite it."

"Ok, then what?"

"I'm not sure, but play helps generate stories."

"That's it! We don't have scales, wings or thick leather skin to protect us, but we do create stories."

"Sure. We swing by our tales."

Everyone groaned at the terrible pun, but one of the hunters had already begun to walk with a strange, bouncing gait. He hunched his shoulders and looked all around with wide eyes, smiling. He then repeated the pattern, moving purposefully and yet at random.

Another hunter crouched down on all fours, like a dog, and began to laugh, cocking his head and looking up and to the left. He then whirled around in circles and scampered off, gleefully.

A third hunter leaped up as high as she could for no reason at all. She kept leaping and leaping. When she tried to twirl in the air as she leaped, she fell, got up and tried again and again.

"I think they are trying to get a story to come out and play," a hunter close to me said with a twinkle in his eye, then he too began to do strange things.

By this time none of the hunters were interested in what I was saying, but I kept on talking anyway. "What if there were no words? Could we see or be anything?" I shouted as they danced, scampered and bounced off together.

"We need to leave our own trail of words," I said to myself. "That's what will attract it to us. We have to tell each other into existence."

We made a strange procession moving through the unusual forest. I began to breathe more quickly as the trail grew steeper. Finally, when I had to stop and rest, the others disappeared.

As I rested I said out loud, "When the action that I am is revealed in story, my 'me' comes into view. As I tell it, my 'I' and my 'me' converse! That discloses identity," I shouted to the others, but they were unable to hear.

I began to climb upward again. The altitude and, perhaps, all my talking, made breathing more difficult. I was vaguely nauseated. "If I stop talking," I mumbled in the thin air, "the hunt will stop." I rounded a huge rock and the thinning forest was gone.

I began to run to catch up, panting heavily as the cold air burned my lungs. I could see the others now above me. They were following something with great intensity. Rocks rattled and bounced down the slope from their hurry. As I watched, a mist slowly gathered, blotting out my friends. I hurried more carefully, following the muffled sound of their voices. Then they were all around me. The mist thinned and I realized we were standing on the peak. The mountain now fell away sharply on all three sides.

I could not speak. I counted the hunters. Some were gone.

"What happened?"

"They just went on."

"Where?"

The others shrugged.

As I caught sight of mountain ranges going on to infinity, I blacked out.

When I awoke clouds were racing at us. Icy rain stung my cheeks. The air buzzed with electricity seeking a place to discharge. Our hair rose and our ice axes began to sing.

"We have to go down."

"What about the others?"

"I don't know. We must go *now*."

We made it to timberline just as the storm broke. Everything turned white as the wind blew snow through the forest. We stopped to open our packs and pulled out our down vests. We zipped up parkas, closing out the wind and cold. Tension began to drain away as we walked down and out through the trees.

The descent was meditative, but gravity seemed to conspire with every stone and exposed root to trip us. Finally, we were at the labyrinth's doorway. We moved through it and out its rings to our camp. A fire was started. As we warmed our hands, the ones who had gone on, no longer needing language, rejoined us one by one.

"Stories can't be caught," someone said. "They catch us!" We all laughed, except for the ones who had just joined us. They looked puzzled.

...and so it is to this day.
...and if you don't believe me I can show you the mountain.
...and the labyrinth lives there still.
...and that is the end of that.
...go and do likewise.
...Amen.

CHAPTER 3

PLAY, PSEUDOPLAY AND GRACE

DARK PLACES AND DUVETS

Our three-year-old Louisa was playing with the Good Shepherd material in our living room. First she played the conventional version of the story, but then she played prolonged adventures of sheep in "dark places," demonstrating a degree of violence and darkness that deeply surprised and shocked me as her mother. Eventually all the sheep were rescued by the shepherd and taken to the sheepfold. The dark places were "sunk" at the bottom of the cool water and so disappeared from view—at which I prickled more. Evil doesn't just "go away," does it?

Well, it must have felt like that to her, so I stayed silent. Now, she said, it was time for the sheep to go to bed. And so began a prolonged going-to-bed routine. Ah, she said, but they need duvets. She fished out the dark felt places, newly "baptized" as duvets! So each sheep received a duvet, and was tucked in by the Good Shepherd, and kissed "good night."

But of course they didn't all go straight to sleep: one wanted another kiss, one wanted a glass of water, another wanted a story tape to help her get off to sleep, another needed the duvet pulled up again, etc. Each time the Good Shepherd showed what he was made of: uncon-ditional love and patience—rather unlike Louisa's real experience of extended bedtimes with her caregivers, who get impatient and tired.

Finally all the sheep were pronounced "asleep." She placed the Good Shepherd outside the gate of the sheepfold. Then she said, looking at the scene she had made, "Oh, the Good Shepherd might feel lonely now. He wishes that sometimes the sheep could wake up and love him back."

If ever there was an argument for the adult onlooker staying silent, to allow the child to play her own way (however unorthodox it gets), I think this experience was it for me. I am certain that any intervention on my part would have prevented Louisa from getting to this ending through her own experience and language. She not only fully came to grips with the relationship of the Shepherd to his sheep, but also began to glimpse the place of response to this love, the two-way nature of this relationship and the challenge of the next step of "loving back."

—Rebecca Nye, Godly Play Trainer

AN ADULT EXPERIENCE OF PLAY

Sometimes I joke that Godly Play is a whole lot more fun to do than to talk about. At the risk of limiting our fun, in this chapter I would like to talk a little about play. Play is a fundamental medium of childhood. To fully enter into Godly Play, we have to be deeply aware of what makes *real* play and what distracts or detracts from it.

In Chapter 1, I invited you to Godly Play: play with God and with the language of the Christian people, through which we come both to know *about* God and to *know* God. In Chapter 2, I affirmed the power of story and invited you to discover your own story and your own calling to be a storyteller. Now it's time to play and to reflect on the meaning of play.

In choosing what to do for play, be careful. So many activities that adults choose for their leisure aren't really play but a kind of working-at play: competing against themselves or others to lower their golf scores or raise their bridge scores. It's not easy to define play, but for the purposes of this exploration, choose an activity that feels like wasting time. Then do that activity, and only that activity, for an entire hour.

That's right. Set aside an hour and waste it. That idea runs counter to everything our busy, pragmatic culture believes in. This exercise is an invitation to discover play by discovering what it is *not*, so don't make any product, don't multitask and don't do anything you feel you "should" do. With play there is no product, but there is deep involvement and deep concentration. You can't do two things at once, because real play entirely engages the player. With play you need to do the activity for your own reasons, not because of anyone's "shoulds," not even your own. Play can't be forced. If you feel you *have* to play—you're not playing.

Try it. Perhaps at first wasting time drives you crazy. Try to stay with it. You may discover that wasting time this way draws you into your own creative process. You may connect with language in a new way, and you may not even want to use language at all, either during your activity or after. For this reason, I'll save reflection questions for the end of this chapter and instead invite you to reflect on the differences between genuine play and pseudoplay. Then I'll extend our reflections to a consideration of what we call "grace" when we are "speaking Christian."

DESCRIBING PLAY

Perhaps you thought setting aside an hour to play was silly. Let's go on, anyway. That's okay. Perhaps the meaning of play will become clear from the words we use to talk about it, and then you will want to try again to play. There are many ways to get from here to there. Let's begin with a question.

"What is shared by mass murderers, felony drunk drivers, starving children, head-banging laboratory animals, some anxious students, most upwardly mobile executives and all reptiles?" Stuart L. Brown's answer to his own question is, "They do not play."[4] (New evidence about reptiles qualifies Brown's remarks.)

Brown, an important researcher and writer about play, then comments on the play behavior of animals in the wild, "Systematic research indicates that play burns up to 20 percent of the survival energy of the young and the growing."[5] This is true despite the risk of death and damage to the participants and despite the fact that play does not actually provide the food, shelter, safety or other outcomes necessary for survival. Why would evolution favor the use of so much biological energy in the service of seemingly useless activity? Perhaps it is not as "useless" as it seems.

To discuss the possibility of play's value we will follow three steps. First, we will consider the ambiguity of play and attempt a "nondefinition." Second, we will analyze pseudoplay, the opposite of play, which has destructive outcomes for those who live by it and those who mistake it for play. Finally, we will examine the continuum of play and pseudoplay together with the continuum of verbal and nonverbal communication to provide a means by which we can evaluate the quality of play in religious education practice, in worship and in our daily lives. We will conclude with the role of theological *grace* in Godly Play and grace's physical, nonverbal connotations.

THE DIFFICULTY OF DEFINING PLAY

I'll divide this discussion of play's ambiguity into two parts: first, a look at play from the scientific point of view; second, a discussion of how theology has approached play's lack of definition. I'll add a footnote about a theology of childhood and play, but reserve the fuller discussion of a theology of childhood for Chapter 7.

SCIENTIFIC AMBIGUITY

When Brian Sutton-Smith wrote *The Ambiguity of Play* after over forty years of formally studying and writing about play and games, he thought that he had at long last "gotten it right." He was able "to bring some coherence to the ambiguous field of play theory by suggesting that some of the chaos to be found there is due to the lack of clarity about the popular cultural rhetorics that underlie the various play theories and play terms."[6]

He defined a "rhetoric" as "a persuasive discourse, or an implicit narrative, wittingly or unwittingly adopted by members of a particular affiliation to persuade others of the veracity and worthwhileness of their beliefs."[7] The seven rhetorics Sutton-

Smith identified are divided into two groups: ancient, community-minded views and modern pragmatic views, arising since about 1800 when play began to be studied in a systematic, scientific way.

The ancient views of play related it to power (status, victory), to fate (magic, luck), to community identity (festivals, cooperation) or to frivolity (nonsense as opposed to work). Modern views, however, see play as involving progress (adaptation, growth), the imaginary (creativity, fantasy) or the concerns of the self (peak experiences, leisure). "In general each rhetoric has a historical source, a particular function, a distinctive lucid form, specialized players and advocates, and is the context for particular academic disciplines."[8]

The ambiguity of play, then, is not the result of its diversity of forms or experiences, the many kinds of players, the variety of play agencies or the multitude of play scenarios. The reason we have no general theory of play is because the study of play has so many different starting points.

However, in addition to play's ambiguity, I would like to add another reason that we have no broad-based definition of play. According to Terrence Deacon, author of *Symbolic Species: The Co-Evolution of Language and the Brain*, humankind has developed the ability for symbolic referencing (that is, the ability for verbal communication), together with iconic and indexical referencing (that is, nonverbal kinds of communication), which is parallel to but independent from verbal communication.

Even though our nonverbal communication systems are independent, however, they still provide the ground for our verbal (symbolic) communication. In other words, *how* we say things provides the context for *what* we say. This "how" comes from our nonverbal communication system.

Since play is signaled by our nonverbal communication system—a smile, the cocking of the head, a twinkle in the eye—we can only partially describe what we do when we play. In fact there is nothing we can say or do in a nonplayful way that we cannot also say or do in a playful way, depending on our gesturing. There is no way to make a one-to-one translation from playing to symbolic referencing, that is, using words to define play. This would be like trying to literally translate crying or laughing into words.

To identify play, then, we need to show it physically rather than reduce it to precise terms. The task of showing play has little similarity to the task of defining such things as triangles, which are useful verbal constructions imposed on nature's complexity. We propose, then, to describe play rather than define it.

In her book *Play*, Catherine Garvey provides an apt and concise description. She writes that play is "pleasurable, has no extrinsic goals, is spontaneous and voluntary, involves active engagement, and has systematic relations to what is not play such as creativity, problem solving, language learning, the development of social roles, and a number of other cognitive and social phenomena."[9]

Garvey's description denotes play's basic qualities. It does not state the precise meaning of the word. This description sets the bounds for the experience that must be shown to fully understand it nonverbally.

Some human beings are better at "showing" play than others. For example, adult artists often retain a special sensitivity to nonverbal communication. They are adept at playing with movement, stone, color, sounds and other media—including words.

Children make up a second group of humans who are especially sensitive to nonverbal communication. They have no choice but to be in tune with their nonverbal systems of communication, since their verbal skills are just developing.

Vestiges of the nonverbal can be found in the verbal by noticing the connotations of our words. According to Howard Gardner, the roots of connotation are in the pre-object-formation ways of knowing.[10] The seven to nine ways in which we create meaning involve connotation in different ways. Connotation communicates by what Gardner calls modes and vectors, a kind of deep body knowing. This probably begins in a global way and then develops more specificity in centers of sensitivity, such as the mouth. Examples of modes and vectors are:

- moving towards and away from
- wholeness and particularity
- being empty or full
- opening and closing

Instead of using denotative language to fashion a definition of play, then, it may be better to use connotative language. Instead of seeking precision, a better approach may be through the ambiguity of poetry. I propose, therefore, a working "non-definition" of play as being graceful, rather than awkward, competent, bored or weary. Play and grace seem to overlap as experiences. Being grace-full versus empty has other connotations, too: valued versus invalid, well versus ill, connected versus disconnected and complex versus either chaotic or rigidly ordered.

We will further discuss play as being graceful by seeking its opposite in a moment. First, however, we need to see what the theology of recent years has had to say about play and why play and grace have not been connected decisively in that discussion.

THEOLOGICAL AMBIGUITY

Interest in a theology of play arose in the late 1960s and early 1970s. It paralleled a rising interest in play among psychologists. David L. Miller's *Gods and Games:*

Toward a Theology of Play provided a concise and creative literature review, as well as a manifesto, for this new way of looking at theology.[11] By the 1980s, however, any discussion of a theology of play had disappeared. Why?

As early as 1972, Jurgen Moltmann summed up the reason for the failing interest in a theology of play. He had taken part in a symposium, which was the basis for the book *Theology of Play.*[12] In a response to the other three participants—Sam Keen, David L. Miller and Robert E. Neale—he said that "the Puritan of work easily changes into the Puritan of play and remains a Puritan."

He also argued that "play" was so broadly defined in the discussion that it included nearly everything, so it meant nothing in particular. This made it impossible to distinguish between good play and bad play. Moltmann went on to say that in the meantime there are still tears of sadness. "Auschwitz remains Auschwitz."[13]

Moltmann raised important questions, but play need not be understood theologically only from the way the discussion was framed by the theology of play advocates. It can also be part of a larger project, which we will call a theology of childhood.

A theology of childhood explores the theme of Jesus' dictum that if we hope to be mature we need to become like children. Almost nothing Jesus directed our attention to about children involved speech, so one clue about entering the Kingdom is that it is not about symbolic referencing, or "getting the words right." Since play is part of our nonverbal communication system we need to consider it as part of what is needed for educating people about becoming mature Christians.

A theology of childhood, as I conceive it, is about our awareness of play's quality— as well as the quality of our other nonverbal communication—so we can keep our nonverbal communication in harmony with our verbal communication. This is so we can communicate in clear and direct ways with God, with others, with nature and with our own deep self. Discord between our verbal and nonverbal communication not only mars our teaching and learning but our whole system of knowing and being in the world.

THE OPPOSITE OF PLAY

We turn now to the second step of our discussion. Perhaps we can clarify our poetic, connotative meaning for play by discussing its opposite. The opposite of play, of course, depends on what we think play is, even if that specification remains at the level of intuition.

I propose that our search for the opposite of play, like our search for a definition of play, will involve connotation (that is, description and intuitive language) rather than denotation (that is, precise definition). This way we can include as much nonverbal, body-based "knowing" as possible in our description. Let's proceed by trial and error.

First, let us try out "seriousness" as the opposite of play. This is a classic proposal and one that Huizinga, the author of *Homo Ludens*, dismissed in the following way: Seriousness seeks to exclude play while play includes seriousness.[14] This makes play a higher order concept than the play-seriousness dichotomy suggests.

What about the common assumption that "work" is the opposite of play? The problem with making a dichotomy of play and work is that for some people their work *is* play. Scientists, artists and many others serve as examples of this exuberant approach. For example, the athlete needs to work at his or her game to play well. Practice brings the player to a new level of integration and play flows again *after* the practice, at a higher level of skill and complexity. This approach sees work and play as two parts of a unified rhythm of life rather than opposites.

What I would like to propose for an opposite to play is *emptiness*. This is somewhat poetic, but as we have already seen such connotative language may be the best way to put play and its opposite into words.

When we are at play, we are full of life, connected to the game and to the players in the game. Synergy abounds. When we cannot play, we are, at best, only maintaining life. One tragic example of this emptiness is that starving and depressed children do not play. They have lost their gracefulness.

In the absence of privation or trauma, human emptiness results primarily from the strong pull of an imperative to feel good without expending energy. The pleasure of this least-effort impulse is ancient. It is probably rooted in the conservation of energy needed to be prepared to face an unexpected danger at any minute and yet avoid burning out from such unrelenting stress.

This concept of emptiness needs to be distinguished from the classical mystical idea of emptiness. The mystic is speaking about making room for God, so what is emptied is self-concern. The presence of God fills up this absence, so in this sense the mystics are not empty. Mystical emptying fills one with an energy of the highest kind, the creative energy of the human creature at play with the Creator.

The emptiness we are referring to as the opposite of play is what haunts energy misers. They are empty, because they isolate themselves from play with the deep self, with others, with nature and with God. Such people are dangerous because they are parasites. They are compelled to suck the life out of others to even appear full of life to themselves and to others.

People who cannot play do not necessarily present themselves as dull. They often appear sparkling and brilliant, because they must be attractive to draw others to them. If this fails they must achieve positions of power so that others can be compelled to be in their company. Either way, attracting or compelling, their aim is to consume the energy of those around them.

It is not surprising that energy sponges have been identified as evil and personified as satanic. They are, indeed, the historical enemies of life. In Hebrew and Greek, for example, "satan" means enemy or adversary. A classic portrayal of an empty one who is glittering with intelligence and attractive power is Milton's Satan in *Paradise Lost*.

Whether you take a positive or negative view of Milton's Satan you still must consider that he is at times lying, deceiving himself or mad. The ambivalence of this figure gives depth and intrigue to the character, but more importantly, Milton has taken seriously the difficulty of discerning the difference between play and pseudoplay in his monumental character.

Another example from literature, more widely read today, is from William Golding's *Lord of the Flies*. The boys stranded on an island build their first civilization around Ralph and his meetings called by the conch shell. He is someone who can play with delight, as the first pages of the novel show.

> Ralph did a surface dive and swam under water with his eyes open; the sandy edge of the pool loomed up like a hillside. He turned over, holding his nose, and a golden light danced and shattered just over his face.[15]

Jack is Ralph's opposite. His play is not play for the sake of play, but is calculated to attract followers. He is an empty one and advocates his leadership at first from the power of position: "because I'm chapter chorister and head boy. I can sing C sharp."[16] He also has a knife and when he learns to hunt and to disguise his face with paint, he opposes Ralph's reasoned and cooperative approach to leadership by an exercise of power, the power of his disguise and violence. He compels others to follow him and tries to disguise what they are doing as play.

Jack's rise to power can be traced in the novel by attending to the quality of laughter and "fun" among the boys. It moves from a sign of play in the leadership of Ralph to a sign of derision in the voice of Jack and his followers. Jack rules by fear, the fear of the leader, reinforced because it protects his followers from a larger fear, "the beast," which he keeps vividly alive in everyone's experience.

When Jack invites Ralph and his few remaining followers to join his tribe he says, "We hunt and feast and have fun. If you want to join my tribe come and see us. Perhaps I'll let you join. Perhaps not."[17] His idea of fun has nothing to do with play, but is only a way to retain power over the others.

Later, Jack makes another invitation to pseudoplay: "Who'll join my tribe and have fun?"[18] This fun involves a frenzied dance of death at night during which Simon—

who has climbed the mountain alone and faced the "beast," a dead man moved about by a parachute in the wind—crawls out of the bushes exhausted after his ordeal.

The other boys are dancing and singing, "Kill the beast! Cut his throat! Spill his blood. Do him in."[19] In their frenzy, perhaps they do not even recognize Simon as they make him the victim of their lust and kill him. That was what "fun" and "play" and "laughter" had come to mean under the rule of the empty one.

There are times when people, who would rather play than fight, must fight against such energy-draining forces and the people who embody them. Life must be guarded against those who can only simulate life, because involvement in any game on their terms is destructive and robs others of life. To help guard against this danger we need to be more specific about our description of pseudoplay, which wants to disguise itself as genuine play. To do this we will use Garvey's description of play to guide our comparison:

PLAY	**PSEUDOPLAY**
Play is pleasurable.	Pseudoplay is numbness, a restless but hollow simulation of life.
Play has no extrinsic goals.	Pseudoplay is parasitic. It destroys the life of the host to maintain its own survival.
Play is spontaneous.	Pseudoplay is obsessed to attract others to claim their energy.
Play requires engagement.	Pseudoplay is detached, but tries to appear involved. It disguises itself to maintain dominance.
Play nourishes such activities as creativity, language learning and learning social roles.	Pseudoplay exploits others for their energy to gain a sense of being alive. Instead of nurturing and supporting creativity in others, it can only rob others of their creativity.

In theological language we might say that true players are aware of God's image as the Creator within them and a closeness between the Creator and the creature at play. For the pseudoplayer the image of God is lost or at least obscured, and there is rebellion against God. Such a person is unable to act and can only react. Theologians have frequently turned to emptiness as a description of evil, from the early Church's description of evil as *privatio boni* (the absence of good) to the *das Nichtige* (the nothingness) of Karl Barth in the twentieth century.

When we take away the mask of pseudoplay, we find evil, the nature and source of which Tom Shippey, the leading interpreter of J. R. R. Tolkien, takes to be "the central issue of *The Lord of the Rings*, as of so many modern fantasies."[20] Tolkien, however, maintains "a running ambivalence" between the counterintuitive, orthodox view, which claims evil is nothing, the absence of the good, and the view of evil as a force which must be resisted. Evil as an absence ("the Shadow") and evil as a force ("the Dark Power") drives much of this plot and "is expressed not only through the paradoxes of wraiths and shadows, but also through the Ring."[21]

The two views of evil are both deeply rooted and irreconcilable. Perhaps we can say that evil is internal, caused by human sin, weakness and alienation from God (the Ring feels heavy to Frodo) and it is experienced also as external (the Ring obeys the will of its master). Evil begins with good intentions and, without resistance, can destroy the holder. This ambiguity is played out at its most intense level between Frodo and Gollum with the added aspect of the Hobbit "luck" of both Bilbo and Frodo who spared Gollum. In Christian language, may we call this "luck" akin to grace?

PLAY, PSEUDOPLAY AND EDUCATION

We now combine our first two discussions—verbal and nonverbal communication with play and pseudoplay—to find a way to evaluate the quality of play in religious education or in other religious settings, such as worship. First, let's look at the relationship between play and the kind of communication we use. Second, we will apply this graphic understanding, together with Garvey's description of play, to analyze four dangerous games often found in teaching and learning.

A lack of concordance between our verbal and nonverbal communication causes profound confusion. This confusion is especially tragic for children, because it teaches them that discord *is* communication. It places children in a double bind so that they are wrong if they respond to what is said and they are wrong if they respond to what is shown. The pain of such discord sometimes overwhelms the need for relationship, and children may withdraw. Their souls can wither and die from such isolation.

Such discord is also tragic for adults. As verbal abilities develop, adults tend to rely more and more on words and overlook their actions and gestures. The roots of words pull away from their ground in the nonverbal. We cannot live in a world limited to words-about-words without becoming insane as individuals or as cultures.

To picture the coordination of communication and play we will use the following illustration:

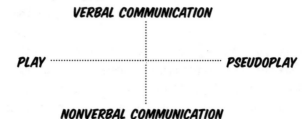

VERBAL COMMUNICATION

PLAY ⋯⋯⋯⋯⋯⋯⋯⋯⋯⋯ **PSEUDOPLAY**

NONVERBAL COMMUNICATION

The horizontal line displays the continuum between play and its opposite pseudoplay. It moves from the overflowing energy of play to the emptiness of pseudoplay. The vertical line shows the relationship of the play continuum to the continuum that runs between verbal and nonverbal communication.

Pseudoplay attempts to disconnect the verbal and the nonverbal. If you listen to the *words*, you hear an invitation to play, but if you read the nonverbal *gestures* and *actions*, the invitation is to pseudoplay. Despite what is being said, the nonverbal signals tell you that this invitation lacks mutuality, spontaneity or other necessary characteristics of genuine play.

The above chart can help us become sensitive to which games in religious education, worship or daily life might be dangerous. I propose four common games we find in such pseudoplay:
• compulsion
• entertainment
• manipulation
• competition

These four games have many overlapping qualities, because they are all examples of pseudoplay.

DANGEROUS GAMES

First, let's look at *compulsion*. In the mid-1960s, Eric Berne catalogued many of these games in his book *Games People Play*.[22] The book touched a responsive chord in its readers, who kept it on the bestseller list for two years. The book's title lives on in the popular vocabulary of our own day.

The "games" Berne describes are compulsive and unconscious. His "play" is actually pseudoplay, since it is not freely chosen. A person, young or old, playing any one of Berne's thirty-two negative games from his "Thesaurus of Games" is stuck in a behavior that is destructive by its very action, because it keeps one stuck, as well as for other reasons.

The only way to get unstuck is to become aware of what game you have been trapped into playing. Instead of "playing tapes" unconsciously, that is, repeating unknowingly a destructive behavior, you can become aware of the game and choose to continue or not. In the fairy tale, the power to make Rumpelstiltskin disappear is found by simply saying his name. Berne, in his enthusiasm for recognizing and naming games, may oversimplify this "Rumpelstiltskin effect." In real life, naming the obsessive game may make us aware of the game, but we almost always need a good bit of work to change the underlying behavior.

When one goes beyond games, Berne wrote, one achieves "jerk-free, game-free conversation between two autonomous Adults."[23] This kind of relationship, which includes what he called "awareness," "spontaneity" and "intimacy" begins to sound more like what we mean by play, but he has described a new, healthy game rather than a nongame. The difference between the two kinds of behavior is the quality of play rather than involvement or noninvolvement in a game.

Religious education is also a game, and the quality of the play by which the game is engaged is critical to what is learned both verbally and nonverbally. The best religious education will display all the characteristics of Garvey's description of play. It will display deep engagement in a voluntary activity done for itself that gives the players pleasure and awakens their creativity, language learning, the learning of social roles and problem-solving abilities.

A second dangerous game is *entertainment*. In entertainment, the energy flows in only one direction. In religious education, the entertainer is a teacher who creates passive consumers out of his or her students. No synergy is possible, since this kind of teaching is about control. One could argue that such a view of teaching begins to empty children of life at an early age rather than stimulating them to play, being filled to overflowing with life.

A third dangerous game is *manipulation*. The teacher directs the activity to produce a product that meets the teacher's needs. Thus the ultimate pleasure in this game is also for the teacher. A child tempted to join such a game will be play-burned by the deception and influenced to avoid future invitations to play. Manipulation is about the needs of the teacher, which means that the learner's links to the pleasure of creativity, language learning, the learning of social roles and problem solving are usually severed.

The fourth dangerous game is *competition*. In this game the teacher competes with the learners or encourages learners to compete with one another. Some spontaneous competition among children may be healthy, but there are some adults who cannot limit competition or stop competing with the children themselves. They must win every time even if it is not in the interest of those who have come to learn. Only the winner has pleasure when pseudoplay dominates, and for every winner there are many losers. The product of this kind of false play is winning and not playing for the play itself. Winning temporarily fills up the empty one, but this craving is never satisfied.

As you can see, these four dangerous games are related: all are for the teacher's needs and all block the children's access to the natural qualities of real play. Furthermore, these are only a few examples of destructive educational games. Pseudoplay is a master of disguises, so such games abound.

When religious education, through nonverbal education, teaches pseudoplay to children, it teaches them that pseudoplay is *normal* for the Christian game. It distorts the players' relationships with their deep selves, with God, with God's creation and with all living creatures because the dysfunctional language taught inevitably shapes the learners' world view.

Play is much more important to religious education than either science or theology have led us to believe. If play dies out among our kind, especially as we struggle with our existential concerns, we will have no creature creative and motivated enough to counter the destructive tendencies of our own species!

GRACE: A DOOR BETWEEN LANGUAGE DOMAINS

Now let's take what we have learned about play and pseudoplay and look at a fundamental Christian word and experience: *grace*. Paul is the champion of grace, having experienced it on the road to Damascus. Saint Augustine followed Paul's thought to make the classical Christian theological statement. Let us take up this discussion by reading two contemporary writers who challenge us with the radical nature of the experience, which, like evil, seems to have an internal and external dimension. These modern champions of grace are Fredric Buechner and Robert Farrar Capon. Both have found the graceful doorway between theology and everyday experience.

Frederick Buechner defined grace in his *Wishful Seeker's: A Theological ABC, Revised and Expanded*. First, he wondered at how this theological word had escaped the centuries of distortion and worn-out usage that had obscured other such terms. Even the words *gracious* and *graceful* "still have some of the bloom left."[24]

As he wrote, "Grace is something you can never get but only be given."[25] This is not something you can deserve or bargain to earn. In the Christian usage of the term there is the somewhat threadbare phrase of "being saved by grace," but one needs to remember that there is nothing that the person "saved" can do. To put it more clearly, still following Buechner:

There is *nothing* you have to do.
There is nothing *you* have to do.
There is nothing you *have* to do.
There is nothing you have to *do*.[26]

Like any other gift, the gift of grace can be yours only if you reach out with open hands and receive it. Of course, reaching out with open hands may be grace as well. The clenched fist of anger or effort will not do! This is a very radical doctrine.

The outrageous quality of grace, to which we might also compare the outrage of "wasting time" in play, is especially well described by Robert Farrar Capon in his book *Between Noon and Three: Romance, Law, and the Outrage of Grace*. Capon wants us to be sure to notice that Romans 5:8 does not say "Christ died for us, on the condition that after a reasonable length of time we would be the kind of people no one would ever have had to die for in the first place. Otherwise, the whole deal is off."[27] There is no deal. There is only grace.

Capon is as passionate about this as Paul is. They both want us to understand that, even if sin continues, *grace still abounds*. The cry of "permissiveness," goes up in a shout, but you can't get away from a love that will not let you go, so we are safe, not safe so long as we behave, but safe without any qualifier. There is nothing that can separate us from the love of Christ, who by the way, yet again, died for the ungodly. Grace is not salvation by moral perfection.

When Jesus says that his yoke is easy and his burden light, he is not kidding. He is not trying to put us down or get us under control. He is meek and lowly in heart, and that is the farthest thing from his mind. What Jesus wants to do is to communicate rest unto our souls. We need to be able to play as well as work.

"There is therefore now no condemnation to them which are in Christ Jesus." This ultimate statement of grace in Romans 8:1 makes people defensive. Why? We are tempted to say that such grace is a nice sentiment, a fantasy, but now it is time to get back to cases of the moral law, the perfection of one's spiritual life or the gritty reality of life in the world. Instead, Paul flatly asserts that grace is unconditional.

What makes us feel defensive is that the unconditional gift of grace also gives us the uncomfortable gift of freedom. You and I are free. Free. What do *you* plan to do? You are "really free. Free forever...Law, Sin, Guilt, Blame—it all rolls off your back like rain off a tombstone,"[28] because the old self is dead, put to death by the graceful presence of Christ mediated by the sacrament of bread and wine, by other people (even the ones we don't like or respect), by the earth and even our deepest selves.

Buechner noted in his definition of justification that:

> At a moment in his life when he had least reason to expect it, Paul was staggered by the idea that no matter who you are or what you've done, God wants you on his side. There is nothing you have to do or be. It's on the house. It goes with the territory. God has "justified you," lined you up. To feel this somehow in your bones is the first step on the way to being saved...just noticing the holy and hallowing givenness of your own life.[29]

Being graceful is a manifestation of God being with us. The result is effortless movement, life play. We are no longer clumsy, trying too hard and stumbling. It is at this graceful point that I would like to suggest that we find play at its most authentic in Godly Play.

Chaos arouses anxiety and stumbling, while being overly-ordered arouses boredom and frustration. The right balance between chaos and rigidity, a different balance in each person, results in a flowing gracefulness that makes one happy in a creative and energetic way. This flow can be conceived in psychological terms, as Csikszentmihalyi has done,[30] or in terms of self-emergent order arising out of chaos, as physics does. It can also be conceived of as play. When play includes God as Trinity—the relationship with the Creator, the Word who creates and recreates us with human words and actions, and the Creator Spirit within—we have graceful Godly Play. We also have an integrating experience which comes from both within and without to make us whole and overcome the evil that fragments us.

REFLECTING: PLAY, PSEUDOPLAY AND GRACE

You might want to pause and reflect on your own experience and understanding of play:

• What was a typical way I played when I was five years old? When I was ten years old? When I was twenty years old? In the last five years?

....

....

....

....

....

- When I was a child, what messages did I hear about play from my parents? from my teachers? From my siblings? from my friends?

  ....
  ....
  ....
  ....
  ....

- Can I identify any pseudoplay that took place in my religious or secular education? What words and actions can I remember from that pseudoplay?

  ....
  ....
  ....
  ....
  ....

- Can I identify any genuine play that took place in my religious or secular education? What words and actions can I remember from that genuine play?

  ....
  ....
  ....
  ....
  ....

- Can I remember one or more experiences of grace in my life? What qualities of play can I now identify in that experience? (If necessary, refer to the five-part description of play on p. 43.)

  ....
  ....
  ....
  ....
  ....

CHAPTER 4

THE NUTS & BOLTS OF GODLY PLAY

BRING GOD TO THE STORY

One Sunday morning during Lent, I told a portion of the story The Faces of Christ to about sixteen children, ages from three to eleven. At the wondering, I asked the children if there was anything in the room that we could bring to the story to help us tell it better. The children brought several objects from the stories on the shelves and placed them by the story on the floor.

Then one little six-year-old boy said, "We could bring God to the story." Amazed at his suggestion, I said, "I wonder how we could bring God to the story?" He replied, "Well, we need to be very quiet and pray." At his suggestion, all the children became quiet and bowed their heads. After a moment of silence, the little boy said, "Amen," and then he said, "God is here." I was then simply a participant with the other children, under the inspired leadership of this child and utterly amazed at their self-directed silence.

—Sharon Greeley, Godly Play Trainer

If you have been enjoying the guided reflections and readings of this book, you may by now have become convinced that play with God is of ultimate importance: the great game worth playing. But how will you *do* Godly Play? It is now time to talk about the nuts and bolts: how to manage time, space and relationships in a Godly Play setting.

In a Godly Play setting, we manage time, so that children who enter the room enter into *kairos* time, time that is both orderly and leisurely. Children who come week after week learn that here no one will rush them. No one will tell them that they have to get their work finished "on time." Godly Play teachers learn to say with conviction, "We have all the time we need." This kind of orderly and leisurely time is the gift mystics throughout the centuries have given themselves to experience their playful prayer with God.

In a Godly Play setting, we manage space, so that children who enter the room find themselves surrounded by the language of the Christian people in all its beautiful, *touchable* richness. The first thing they see, right across from the doorway, are the focus shelves with the Holy Family, the Risen Christ, the baptismal Light and the Good Shepherd with his sheep. Other shelves hold the sacred stories of God's

People and golden boxes of parables, each a world of its own. Everything is within the children's reach to proclaim, without a word, "This place, and everything in it, is for you. You belong here."

In a Godly Play setting, we nourish relationships—that is, we manage ourselves in order to support healthy relationships in the children's community. Children who enter the room experience a place where they are accepted for who they are, not manipulated to win an adult's praise or approval. Through repeated actions and responses that offer invitation, respect and empowerment, the children come to experience the ethics of God's People lived out in every interaction. The message we give is, "You are capable. You can choose your own materials and take good care of them. You can clean up your own spills. You can ask someone to share, and you can take no for an answer. You can make good choices. You are a responsible, beloved member of this community."

In Chapter 5, we'll explore different settings in which Godly Play can be used, but in this chapter we'll explore its most typical setting: the religious education classroom, a specially prepared space in which two teachers guide the session, making time for the children:

- to enter the space and be greeted
- to prepare themselves for the presentation
- to enter into a presentation based on a parable, sacred story or liturgical action
- to respond to the presentation through shared wondering
- to respond to the presentation (or other significant spiritual issues) with their own work, either expressive art or with the lesson materials
- to prepare and share a feast
- to say goodbye and leave the space

To help understand what Godly Play *is*, we can also take a look at what Godly Play is *not*. First, Godly Play is *not* a complete children's program. Christmas pageants, vacation Bible school, children's choirs, children's and youth groups, parent-child retreats, picnics, service opportunities and other components of a full and vibrant children's ministry are all important and are not in competition with Godly Play. What Godly Play contributes to the glorious mix of activities is what is important: the art of knowing how to use the language of the Christian People to make meaning about life and death.

Godly Play is different from many other approaches to children's work with scripture. One popular approach is having fun with scripture. That's an approach we might find in many church school pageants, vacation Bible schools, musicals and other children's activities. A family needs to be silly together sometimes, so having fun with scripture is fine, but children also need *respectful* experiences with scripture if they are to fully enter into its power. If we leave out the heart of the matter, we risk trivializing the Christian way of life and making its language superficial.

HOW DO YOU DO GODLY PLAY?

In ancient times, the Bible was not a book. It was stories, often told around a camp-fire. The children snuggled in with their extended families. The cold and dark were pushed away by the light and warmth of the fire and the community. The children listened, even if half asleep, to the elders' tales. They learned how to do this by custom. Today children are more used to flipping stations on a television set. The ability to listen deeply with wonder is becoming lost. We need to teach this again, so let's explore now how Godly Play does this in a step-by-step way.

When doing Godly Play, *be patient*. With time, your own teaching style, informed by the practices of Godly Play, will emerge. Even if you use another curriculum for church school, you can begin to incorporate aspects of Godly Play into your practice —beginning with elements as simple as the greeting and goodbye.

Pay careful attention to the environment you provide for children. The Godly Play environment is an "open" environment in the sense that children may make genuine choices regarding both the materials they use and the process by which they work toward shared goals. The Godly Play environment is a "boundaried" environment in the sense that children are guided to make their own choices within constructive limits.

As teachers, we set nurturing boundaries for the Godly Play environment by managing *time, space* and *relationships* in a clear and firm way.

HOW TO MANAGE TIME

AN IDEAL SESSION

In its research setting, a full Godly Play session takes about two hours. However, church schools might provide as little as forty-five minutes for a single session. First we'll describe an ideal session, then make suggestions for the "forty-five-minute hour." An ideal session has four parts, each part echoing the way most Christians organize their worship together:

OPENING: ENTERING THE SPACE AND BUILDING THE CIRCLE
At the Doorway
The storyteller sits in the circle, waiting for the children to enter. The door person helps children and parents separate at the doorway, and helps the children slow down as they enter the room. Encourage parents to stay outside the room, so that the room itself can be kept child-centered. (You'll find a helpful handout for parents that will explain Godly Play principles to them in *The Complete Guide to Godly Play, Volume 2*.)

The door person greets each child warmly, then asks, "Are you ready?" This begins the dialogue we want to offer each child in every Godly Play session. We *invite* the child to enter, and let the child decide within limits whether or not he or she is ready to enter. When the child is ready, the door person can say, "Good. Walk very carefully to the circle, and the storyteller will help you find just the right place to sit."

When the children have entered, and it is time for the lesson to begin, the door person closes the door. (If there are support people who bring supplies for the feast, the door person puts a note on the door with the count of children for that day's feast.) If children arrive later, the door person supports them while they sit by the door until after the lesson and wondering questions are finished. At that time, the children who were late can go to the storyteller for their own wondering.

On the other hand, the door person may know that a particular child will most likely be able to enter the circle without disturbing the lesson or wandering. That child is sent directly and quietly on to join the circle.

Building the Circle

As the child comes to the circle, the storyteller helps each child find a good place to sit. Your knowledge of the children's needs will help you build a circle effectively. If there are children who find it easy to get ready and to stay focused, put them in places where they can help model these behaviors for the circle: directly across from you or right next to you. If there are children who need extra support in getting ready and staying focused, find places for them that are close to you, but not directly next to you, so you can see them.

Take your time in greeting children and helping them find their places. Listen for their news, and enjoy the pleasures of "small talk" as you build the circle. When the door person closes the door, help the children get ready for the day's lesson. "It's time to get ready for our story." Show children how to sit with their legs crossed and their hands folded at the ankles. Will young children keep this position for long? No. But it *is* a position they can practice and return to whenever you say, "It's time to get ready." When the children are ready, the storyteller pauses to breathe and get centered before beginning the story.

HEARING THE WORD OF GOD: PRESENTATION, WONDERING AND RESPONSE

Presentation

On the wall there is a large Circle of the Church Year wall hanging with an arrow that points to the different colors of the Church year. The storyteller first invites a child to move the hand of this Church "clock" to the next block of color. (Sometimes when seasons have unpredictable numbers of weeks, such as the season after Christmas, the storyteller needs to prepare the clock *before* the session by moving the hand to the block *before* the correct color for today's session.)

If the color is a new one, showing a change of season, the storyteller will then change the color of cloth under the Holy Family. (This presentation is repeated in each of *Volumes 2-4*.) This draws the children's attention to the Holy Family, in the center of the top shelf of the focus shelves behind the storyteller.

Then the storyteller presents the day's lesson: a sacred story, a parable or a liturgical action, according to the calendar and the storyteller's preparation. If the storyteller is unprepared, it's better to offer the children a work session or retell a story that is well-known than to read an unfamiliar story from a prepared script. If you read the lesson, you show that the real lesson is the writing on the paper, and that the presentation is not lived by you.

The storyteller begins by saying, "Watch where I go to get this lesson." Even if the lesson is right behind you, it's better to walk around the room looking for the lesson and describing what you're doing. This models for the children the process of finding a particular lesson. "Let's see...these are gold parable boxes, it's not here...here are the Books of the Bible...ah, here it is, on the sacred story shelves." If the storyteller needs a rug, she or he gets one from the rug box, hugging it and saying, "We hug our rugs, because we love our work so much."

During the story, the storyteller keeps his or her eyes focused on the materials— not on the children. This is different from some traditions in storytelling, where the storyteller looks into the listeners' eyes throughout. In Godly Play, the storyteller and children both enter as fully as possible into the story it embodies. Keeping your own eyes on the material in the center of the circle will help you "disappear" into the story it embodies. (An exception might be when handling disruptions in the circle. See below: "How to Respond Effectively to Disruptions in the Circle," p. 69.)

Wondering

At the presentation's end, the storyteller sits quietly to enjoy the story that has been laid out, and then raises his or her eyes to focus now on the relationship with the children. The storyteller invites the children to wonder together about the lesson. "I wonder what part of this story you like best?" is one example of a wondering question. There are no predetermined answers to a wondering question. As Godly Play teachers our job is to support the process of wondering, not to approve or disapprove of specific answers. The children's wondering emerges out of their own lives, their relationship with God and their participation in the lesson. Let God be there. Allow this powerful language to do its work. Trust the searching of the children to find what they need with God and the scriptures.

Each kind of presentation (sacred stories, parables and liturgical actions) has its own type of wondering questions. Sacred stories are stories that invite us to claim our identity as one of God's People. An important wondering question for sacred stories is, "I wonder where you are in this story, or what part of this story is about you?" Parables are brief narratives that challenge our everyday view of life. An important wondering question for parables is, "I wonder what this seed (pearl, tree, etc.) could really be?" Liturgical action presentations invite us to integrate our life with the worship of the Christian people. An important wondering question for liturgical actions is, "I wonder if you have ever come close to this color (water, light, etc.) in church?"

Depending on the age and personalities of the children or the mood of the lesson, you may hear many responses to wondering questions or almost none. Children may be wondering silently without wanting to speak aloud. Don't hurry the wondering process, and don't worry that you have failed if there is much silence. Silence is also a profound part of the Christian language system, so it is appropriate to experience it in a Godly Play classroom and to be comfortable with it.

When the wondering is finished, the storyteller puts away the material, always modeling his or her love and respect for the materials. Then the storyteller helps the children choose their work for the day. This deeply playful "work" expands on their response, both to the lesson and to the other events in their lives.

Response

The storyteller goes around the circle asking each child to choose work for the day. Children may choose to work with a story they have already heard, to work with art materials, to finish a project begun in an earlier session, to work with cleaning materials or even to take a nap. (In fact, if you've noticed that one child is sleepy, you can encourage that child to take a rug and find a place to rest.)

Children who know what they want to do are dismissed from the circle, one at a time, to get out their work. If a child isn't sure yet, support his or her thoughtfulness by saying, "You can take more time to think about what you want to do. I'll come back to you." Support the children who are waiting for their turn to ask, too. "Waiting can be hard work. You are doing a good job waiting. Think about what you will choose when it is your turn."

The door person supports the children as they get out their work, either storytelling materials, art supplies or cleaning supplies. The door person doesn't get out the work *for* the children, but is ready to model competence and support a child who is learning how to handle the paints or the feather duster. As the children work, some might remain with the storyteller who presents another lesson to them. This smaller group is made up by those who aren't able to choose work on their own yet.

SHARING THE FEAST: PREPARING THE FEAST AND SHARING IT IN HOLY LEISURE

When it is almost time for the feast, the storyteller goes to the light switch and turns the lights off, a quiet unobtrusive signal to the children. "Let me see your eyes. Good. I need to talk to everyone all at once. It's time to put your work away. You don't need to hurry, but you need to put it away now. When you are finished, come to the circle so we can have our feast." Then the storyteller turns the lights back on. (If the room has no natural daylight, turn off only one light for this signal, not all the lights.)

The storyteller usually remains in the circle, then, to welcome the children back, one by one, for the feast. The door person supports the children as they clean up their work and put it away. Again, the door person doesn't do this work *instead of* the children, but helps the children learn the procedures of the room for themselves.

The "feast people" for the Godly Play program should now have a cart outside the door with the day's feast ready on it: a tray of cups, half-filled with juice; a plate of snacks and a basket of napkins. The door person helps three children set out the feast for the children to share.

One server spreads out a napkin in front of each child. Another server places a cup of juice in front of each child. A third server places the snack (crackers, fruit, bread or cookies) in front of each child. A child who does not want something that is being served says, "No, thank you." You need not offer a replacement snack, but children who do not want the day's juice could have a cup of water instead.

The storyteller supports the children in waiting until everyone is served and prayers have been said. "That's right. We will wait for everyone. A feast is more fun when we all share it together." The storyteller invites prayers from the children, but supports their right to choose what kind of prayer to say (silently or aloud), or whether they want to pray at all. Encourage children to end their choice by saying aloud "Amen," so you know it's time for the next child. Finally, pray yourself. I always pray, "Thank you, God, for these wonderful children and for our feast. Amen."

After the feast, children clean up by putting their napkins into their cups, being careful to keep the crumbs inside the napkins. Each child in turn then walks to a trash basket to put his or her cup inside, and returns to the circle to end the session.

DISMISSAL: SAYING GOODBYE AND LEAVING THE SPACE

The door person takes the lead in helping the children leave by looking to see which parents are ready outside the room and which children are ready inside the room. When a parent has arrived for a child who is ready, the door person says that name softly.

The storyteller holds out two hands for that child and invites him or her to say goodbye. The child chooses whether or not to take the hands, give a hug or simply say goodbye without touching. The storyteller can say something like, "It was wonderful to have you here today. It made me happy just to see your face. Come back when you can."

The door person reminds children who forget to return to the storyteller for a goodbye. The children may or may not say goodbye to the door person in their eagerness to rejoin their parents.

This is the end of the session for the children, but ideally the storyteller and door person will, at least occasionally, spend more time together in the room. This investment of time will deepen and enrich the program. First each teacher sits quietly and reflects on the session as a whole. Then each teacher takes time to make notes on the lesson. Apart from ordinary record-keeping, such as noting down the names of children who heard the day's story, teachers can record their impressions of challenging moments and moments to treasure. Finally, they can share their impressions and evaluate the session. What worked well? What could be done differently in a future session?

IF YOU ONLY HAVE A FORTY-FIVE-MINUTE "HOUR" FOR RELIGIOUS EDUCATION

In the research setting, the opening, presentation of the lesson and wondering aloud together about the lesson might take about half an hour. The children's response to the lesson through expressive art, retelling with the materials and other work might take about an hour. The preparation for the feast, the feast and saying goodbye might take another half an hour.

In the more typical religious education setting, however, you will probably have a limited time for your sessions—as little as forty-five minutes instead of two hours. With forty-five minutes, you have several choices:

FOCUS ON THE FEAST

Sometimes children take especially long to get ready. If you need a full fifteen minutes to build the circle, you can move directly to the feast, leaving time for a leisurely goodbye. You will not shortchange the children. The quality of time and relationships that the children experience within the space *is* the most important lesson presented in a session of Godly Play.

FOCUS ON THE WORD

Most often, you will have time for a single presentation, including time for the children and you to respond to the lesson by wondering together. Finish with the feast and then the goodbye ritual. Because the children will have no time to make a work response, we suggest that every three or four sessions, you omit any presentation and focus on the work instead (see directly below).

FOCUS ON THE WORK

If you must usually pass from the presentation directly to the feast, then every three or four sessions, substitute a work session for a presentation. First build the circle. Then, without making a presentation, help children choose their work for the day. Allow enough time at the end of the session to share the feast and say goodbye.

PLANNING THE CHURCH YEAR

We've simplified annual planning by presenting the lessons in their suggested seasonal order of presentation.

In Fall, an opening session on the Church year is followed by Old Testament stories, from creation through the prophets. In Winter, we present the season of Advent and the Feasts of Christmas and Epiphany, followed by the parables. In spring, we present the faces of Christ during Lent, followed by Easter presentations, preparation for Pentecost, the Eucharist and the early Church.

Not all groups will—or should!—follow this suggested order. Some possible exceptions:
- Groups with regularly scheduled short sessions will need to substitute work sessions for presentations every third or fourth Sunday.
- If the storyteller is not yet comfortable with a particular presentation, we recommend substituting a work session for that day's presentation.
- Within a work session, one child might request the repetition of an earlier presentation. Another child might ask a question that suggests an enrichment

presentation; for example, "Why do we have crosses in church?" That's a "teachable moment" to bring out the object box of crosses.

Volumes 2, 3 and *4* of *The Complete Guide to Godly Play* all offer sample schedules for the seasons they cover. Refer to these volumes as you plan your Church year.

HOW TO MANAGE SPACE

GETTING STARTED

To start, focus on the relationships and actions that are essential to Godly Play, rather than on the materials needed in a fully equipped Godly Place space. Not every parish can allocate generous funds for Christian education, but I believe Godly Play is worth beginning with the simplest of resources. Without any materials at all, two teachers can make a Godly Play space that greets the children, shares a feast and blesses them goodbye each week. With materials for one story and a few cans of crayons or markers, the teachers can present a full Godly Play session.

When I began teaching Godly Play, all I had was an empty room. In it I placed a yellow, painted board on the floor, cinder blocks on that and another board to make a set of shelves. In the middle of the top shelf was a shoe box with figures for the parable of the Good Shepherd that I had cut from cardboard. (I still have those cut-outs and I still use them!) I spray painted the box gold, so it wouldn't look like a shoebox, but the print bled through the paint. I painted it again and told the story.

The next week I had made a circle of the Church year from construction paper. The third week I didn't have time to make a new material, so I did the parable of the Good Shepherd again. Over the year, I filled those shelves with more homemade lesson materials. Gradually, as more time and money became available, I upgraded the materials to ones cut from foamcore. Now the room I use in Houston for a Godly Play research room is fully equipped with the beautiful, wooden Godly Play materials, but the most important *start* of a successful Godly Play environment is the nurturing of appropriate relationships in a safe space.

If you are just beginning Godly Play in your church, you have to consider a range of key decisions. Some churches want to plunge right in with fully-equipped rooms. Other churches start more cautiously by using the Godly Play classroom management style together with whatever curriculum is already in place. Over time, they incorporate more elements and materials into their program until they have made the transition to full Godly Play programs.

Those who are beginning a new Godly Play program for their church can use the checklist provided to guide their planning.

PLANNING FOR GODLY PLAY

Use this checklist as you plan your Godly Play program.

STUDENTS

- [ ] age group(s)
- [ ] expected average attendance
- [ ] number of classes/groups

TEACHERS

- [ ] storytellers
- [ ] door persons
- [ ] substitutes
- [ ] training/support needed

SUPPORT PERSONS

- [ ] supply people
- [ ] feast people
- [ ] materials people (carpenters, artists, etc.)

ROOMS

- [ ] exclusive or shared?
- [ ] lighting
- [ ] wall color
- [ ] carpet
- [ ] window coverings
- [ ] shelf units
- [ ] rug box
- [ ] storage for children's work (2-D projects, e.g. paintings, and 3-D projects, e.g. sculptures)

STORIES

- [ ] On what weeks will classes be held?
- [ ] What stories will we tell? When?
- [ ] On what weeks will we have work sessions only?
- [ ] What materials will we purchase? Make?
- [ ] How will we store materials?

SUPPLIES

- [ ] for written work
- [ ] for art responses (paint, clay, markers, etc.

- [ ] cleaning items
- [ ] storage containers
- [ ] trays
- [ ] rugs

FEAST SUPPLIES

- [ ] paper goods (cups, napkins)
- [ ] juices
- [ ] crackers
- [ ] fruit
- [ ] special items

BUDGET

- [ ] room decor/furnishings
- [ ] story materials
- [ ] trays/baskets (for stories)
- [ ] rugs/trays (for children to work with)
- [ ] feast items
- [ ] supplies
- [ ] teacher training
- [ ] gifts (Christmas, Easter, promotion, etc.)
- [ ] miscellaneous items

FUNDS

- [ ] church budget
- [ ] gifts/contributions
- [ ] fund raisers
- [ ] donated labor, materials, items

ADMINISTRATION

- [ ] coordinator
- [ ] committee

PROMOTION

- [ ] relationship to church
- [ ] introduce/promote to:
  - — parents and grandparents
  - — children
  - — community

MATERIALS

MATERIALS FOR PRESENTATIONS

In *Volumes 2, 3* and *4* of *The Complete Guide to Godly Play*, the beginning of each lesson lists the materials you need, then explores the materials in greater detail in a section titled Notes on the Materials.

There are a few materials you will need for *all* seasons, Fall, Winter and Spring:
• the Circle of the Church Year wall hanging
• a set of crèche figures (also called *The Holy Family*, including a baby Jesus detach-able from the crib with arms outstretched, a manger, Mary, Joseph, a shepherd, one or more sheep, a donkey, a cow and the three kings)
• cloths in liturgical colors (white, purple or blue, red, green)
• a figure of the risen Christ with extended arms

You can make any or all of these materials yourself, or purchase beautifully crafted and long-lasting lesson materials from:

> Godly Play Resources
> P.O. Box 563
> Ashland, KS 67831
> (800) 445-4390
> fax: (620) 635-2191
> *www.godlyplay.com*

MATERIALS FOR CHILDREN'S WORK

Gather art supplies that the children can use to make their responses. These materials are kept on the art shelves. We suggest:
• paper in two sizes (9" x 12" and at least 18" x 24")
• painting trays (easy-to-clean, with sides)
• paint and brushes
• smocks
• drawing boards
• crayons, pencils and markers
• boards for modeling clay
• clay rolled into small balls in airtight containers
• basket of wood scraps
• basket of various kinds of cloth
• glue sticks and small bottle of liquid glue

Drawing

Drawing materials include drawing paper, colored felt markers, crayons, colored pencils and pencils. Children who want to draw need drawing boards and their choice of drawing material. Provide a can filled with a set of markers or crayons in a range of colors to each child.

Paints

Paints can be "big paints" (tempera) or "little paints" (watercolors). Each has their own routine for setup and cleanup.

Store *big paints* in lidded paint cups with holes in the tops for the brushes. Keep big brushes for these paints in a basket. A child who wants to work with big paints first gets a rug from the rug box, and then a plastic paint tray. On the tray, the child puts several different colors of paint cups and puts a brush into each cup. Finally, the child needs paper to put on the tray and a painting smock.

When cleaning up big paints, the child first puts away the paints and painted picture, then gets a cleaning set (plastic mat, bucket, pitcher, sponge and cloth) from the cleaning shelves. The child puts the plastic mat down beside the tray and the bucket on the mat. The child uses the pitcher to fill the bucket to a premarked place, then dips the sponge into the bucket as often as necessary to wash the tray clean. Finally the child uses a cloth to dry the tray and puts away the cleaning supplies.

The term *little paints* refers to containers of watercolors, six or eight pans in a strip. Keep little brushes for these paints in their own basket. A child who wants to work with little paints first gets a rug from the rug basket, then a painting tray. On the tray, the child places a strip of paints, a little brush, a container of water and paper. While painting, the child changes the water as often as necessary to keep the painting clear.

Clay

Clay is rolled into small balls so that a child won't use all the clay in the container for one project. A clay board to work on is also needed. Clay projects can be air-dried or, with some kinds of clay, oven-dried to harden. The clay needs to dry white so it can be painted with vivid colors.

Finally, the art materials need to be varied and attractive, so the children's expressive art will not be inhibited by too small a selection of media or an unclear or unattractive display. A beautiful display of materials calls to them to come and play.

MATERIALS FOR THE FEAST

You will need:
- basket of napkins
- serving basket
- cups (to be filled by an adult)
- tray (for the cups, carried by a child)
- pitcher (to fill the cups)
- water (for those who don't want juice)
- snacks (fruit, crackers, cookies, etc.)

MATERIALS FOR CLEANUP

Gather cleaning materials that the children can use to clean up after their work and to care for their environment. We suggest:

• paper towels
• feather duster
• brush and dustpan
• cloths (stored in a clean basket and a dirty basket)
• a tray of sponges and spray bottles with water
• trash can with liner
• a repair kit (sandpaper and glue in a basket)
• a tray of polishing liquid or wool and polishing cloths
• watering can for room plants

Cleanup work that the children can do includes dusting shelves and materials, watering plants, washing cleanup cloths and spraying washable surfaces with water before wiping them down. This work is not only pleasurable for some children, but an important way for children to enter into stewardship tasks. The classroom is a small world. How will children learn to take care of the bigger world outside if we don't help them be good stewards here?

HOW TO ARRANGE MATERIALS

The materials are arranged to communicate visually and silently the language system of the Christian faith: our sacred stories, parables, our liturgical actions and silence. Main presentations are generally kept on the top shelves. Enrichment presentations are generally kept on the second shelves. Bottom shelves are kept free for supplemental materials, such as books, maps or other resources. Separate shelves hold supplies for art, cleanup and the feast. A shelf for children's work in progress is also very important.

Standard Shelf

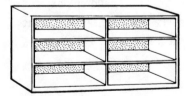

29" (H) x 12" (D) x 60" (W)

Transition Shelf

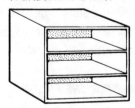

29" (H) x 25" (D) x 24½" (W)

Focal Shelf

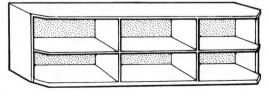

25" (H) x 18¼" (D) x 96" (W)

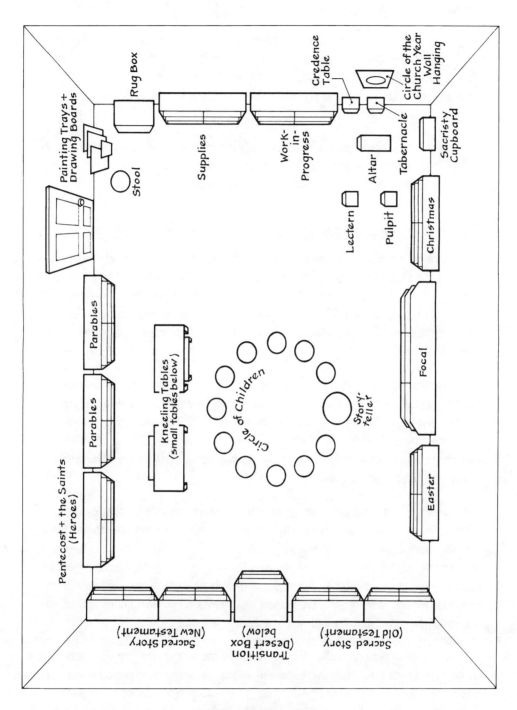

WHERE TO FIND MATERIALS

HOW TO MANAGE RELATIONSHIPS

Of course, we don't really manage relationships. Time management experts say that we don't manage time, we manage ourselves with respect to time. Similarly, when we talk about managing relationships we talk about ways we manage our preparation, tasks and responses in order to provide a safe, consistent environment for the community of children.

All of so-called classroom management is really the support of the community of children. It removes as many of the setups for misbehavior as possible so each child will leave feeling competent, confident and deeply happy.

THE TWO TEACHING ROLES: DOOR PERSON AND STORYTELLER

Each teaching role primarily fosters respect for the children and the Godly Play space. For example, parents are left at the threshold of the Godly Play space and teachers remain at the children's eye level. Both practices keep the room child-centered, instead of adult-centered. (Some day you will be sitting on the floor and an adult will come into the room. Suddenly, you will realize where all the children's stories about giants come from!)

Similarly when the storyteller presents a lesson, he or she keeps eye focus on the materials of the lesson—not the children. Instead of being encouraged to respond to a teacher, the children are invited, by the storyteller's eyes, to enter the story. Throughout the session, the storyteller "anchors" the circle of children, whether they are getting ready, entering into the story, wondering together, choosing work, sharing the feast or saying goodbye.

The teacher whose place is by the door is hard to name, because he or she does many different things to help the Godly Play process move forward. The theme these activities have in common is *thresholds*. This person's contribution has much to do with transitions—entering the room, leaving the circle to get out work, laying out and entering into expressive art, engaging with a chosen lesson, putting work away, preparing for and serving the feast, putting feast things away, cleaning up spills, caring for the room, saying goodbye and leaving the room.

Naming the door person is difficult because his or her task is clearly much more than being a greeter or supporting the hospitality of the feast. The door person is not "the heavy" or the "cop." "Doorway person" or "threshold person" are cumbersome, and even silly, names. I choose "door person" as merely good enough for right now. Someday we will find the right name for this role. Perhaps you will discover it!

In a typical Sunday morning session, only two adults will be present in the Godly Play space: the door person and the storyteller. These are their respective tasks during a typical session:

DOOR PERSON

Check the shelves, especially the supply shelves and art shelves.

Get out the roll book, review notes and get ready to greet the children and parents.

Slow down the children coming into the room. You may need to take and put aside toys, books and other distracting objects. Help them to get ready. Take the roll or have the older children check themselves in.

Close the door when it is time. Be ready to work with latecomers and children who come to you from the circle.

Avoid casual eye contact with the story-teller to help prevent the adults in the room from turning the children into objects, talking down to them or manipulating them.

When the children choose their work, listen so that you can help them get out their work. They may need help setting up artwork and getting materials from the shelves for work on a lesson, either alone or in a group.

Stay in your chair unless children need your help. Do not intrude on the community of children. Stay at the eye level of the children whenever possible, as if there is a glass ceiling in the room at the level of the taller children.

STORYTELLER

Check the material to be presented that day.

Get seated on the floor in the circle and prepare to greet the children.

Guide the children to places in the circle where they will best be able to attend to the lesson. Visit quietly until it is time to begin and all are ready.

Present the lesson. Model how to "enter" the material.

Draw the children into the lesson by your introduction. Bring your gaze down to focus on the material when you begin the actual lesson. Look up when the wondering begins, or if there is a disruption or interruption that requires your attention.

After the lesson and wondering, go around the circle, dismissing each child to begin his or her work, one at a time, as each child chooses what to do. Go quickly around the circle the first time, returning to the children who did not decide. Go around the circle for decisions until only a few are left—who may be new or for some other reason cannot make a choice. Present a lesson to these children.

Remain seated in the circle unless children need help with the lessons they have gotten out. You may need to help with art materials. Keep yourself at the children's eye level when you help.

DOOR PERSON

Help the children put their work away themselves, and also help the children who are getting ready to lay out the feast.

Sit quietly in your chair, but be sure that the trash can has a liner in it. Support the children's careful depositing of things there. "Why, we never have slam dunks here!"

Greet the parents and begin to whisper the names of the children whose parents are there and who are ready.

If a child starts for the door without saying goodbye to the storyteller, remind him or her to return to the storyteller to say goodbye.

Remember to give back anything that may have been taken at the beginning of class.

When the children are gone, check the art and supply shelves and clean.

Sit quietly and contemplate the session as a whole.

Evaluate, make notes and discuss the session with your coteacher.

STORYTELLER

When it is time for the feast, go to the light switch and turn it off. Ask the children to put their work away and come back to the circle for the feast. Turn the light back on. Go to the circle to anchor it as the children finish their work and return.

Ask for prayers, but do not pressure. The feast is also a good time to visit, or to memorize the Lord's Prayer or Psalm 23, just by repeating them. There is not much time, but singing a simple, repetitive song, like a Taize chant, is appropriate. After the feast, show the children how to put their things away in the trash.

Help the children get ready to have their names called.

As the children's names are called, they come to you. Hold out your hands. Children can take your hands, give a hug or keep their distance, as they like. Tell them quietly and privately how glad you were to see them and what good work they did today. Invite them to come back when they can.

Take time to enjoy saying goodbye, with all the warmth of a blessing for each child.

When all are gone, check the material shelves and clean.

Sit quietly and contemplate the session as a whole.

Evaluate the session, make notes and discuss the session with your coteacher.

HOW OTHERS CAN HELP

Other adults who want to support the work of a Godly Play space can contribute by:

- taking turns providing festive and healthy food for the children to share during their feasts
- keeping the art and supply shelves replenished with fresh materials
- using their creative skills to make Godly Play materials for presentation

HOW TO RESPOND EFFECTIVELY TO DISRUPTIONS IN THE CIRCLE

You always want to model the behavior you expect in the circle: focused on the lesson and respectful of everyone in the circle. If a disruption occurs, you deal with that disruption in such a way that you still show continual respect for everyone in the circle—including the child who is having trouble that day. You also still maintain as much focus on the lesson as you can, returning to complete focus on the lesson as quickly as possible, just where you left off. (The lesson remains "suspended" while you deal with the disruption.)

As you consider responses, remember to keep a neutral tone in your voice. Remember, too, that our goal is to help the child move himself or herself toward more appropriate behavior. At the first level of interruption, you might simply raise your eyes from the material. You look up and move your eyes around the circle, looking at each child, while saying, "We need to get ready again. Watch. This is how we get ready." Model the way to get ready and begin again the presentation where you left off.

If the interruption continues or increases, look at the child directly. "No, that's not fair. You need to be ready, too. Let's try again. Good. That's the way."

If the interruption continues or increases, ask the child to sit by the door person. Don't think of this as a punishment or as an exclusion from the story: some children *want* to sit by the door person for their own reasons. Continue to keep a neutral tone of voice as you say, "(*Child's name*), get up and walk carefully over to (*door person's name*). It will be easier for you to get ready there. You can see and hear. The lesson is still for you."

The goal is for the child to take himself or herself to the door. If the child is having trouble, or says, "No!", you can say. "May I help you?" Only if necessary do you gently pick up the child or, in some similar way, help him or her go to the door person.

Of course, not all ages nor even all small children are portable. Suppose you are dealing with a belligerent twelve-year-old taller than you whose only way of relating to adults is by a power struggle. He or she has only one card to play. Say, "Oh, but it will still be easier for you to get ready there." Keep the tone of voice still neutral and relaxed. Then say, "You don't need to wait for me to invite you. You can always go over there when you need to." You then go on with the lesson and let the polarized situation drop of its own weight. Don't feed it with more of your attention.

HOW TO SUPPORT THE CHILDREN'S WORK

We show respect for the children's work in two key ways: through the structure of the classroom in which the children work and through the language we use—and do *not* use—in talking about their work. Let's explore each of these.

CLASSROOM STRUCTURE

A Godly Play classroom is structured to support children's work in four ways:

- First, it makes *materials* inviting and available by keeping the room open, clean and well-organized. A useful phrase for a Godly Play room is, "This material is for you. You can touch this and work with it when you want to. If you haven't had the lesson, ask one of the other children or the storyteller to show it to you." Children walking into a Godly Play classroom take delight in all the fascinating materials calling out to them. These materials say, "This whole room is for you."

- Second, it encourages responsible *stewardship* of the shared materials by helping children learn to take care of the room themselves. When something spills, we could quickly wipe it up ourselves. Instead, by helping children learn to take care of their own spills, we communicate to them the respect we have for their own problem-solving capabilities. At the end of work time, each child learns to put away materials carefully. In fact, some children may want to choose cleaning work—dusting or watering plants—for their entire response time.

- Third, it provides a respectful *place* for children's work by reserving space in the room for both ongoing and finished projects. When a child is still working on a project at the end of work time, reassure him or her by saying, "This project will be here for you next week. You can take as many weeks as you need to finish it. We never lose work in a Godly Play room." Sometimes children want to give a finished piece of work to the room. Sometimes children want to take either finished or unfinished work home. These choices are theirs to make, and ours to respect.

- Fourth, it sets a leisurely *pace* that allows children to engage deeply in their chosen responses. It's better to do no more than build the circle, share a feast and lovingly say goodbye when we are pressed for time than to rush through a story or hurry the response time. When we tell a story, we want to allow enough time for leisurely wondering together. When we provide work time, we want to allow enough time for children to become deeply engaged in their work. In their wondering or their work, children may be dealing with deep issues—issues that matter as much as life and death. Provide them a *safe space* filled with *safe time* for this deep work.

USING LANGUAGE

You can also support children with the language you use:

- Choose *"open" responses*. We choose "open" responses when we simply describe what we see, rather than evaluate the children or their work. Open responses invite children's interaction, but respect children's choices to simply keep working in silence, too. *Examples of open responses:*
  — Hm. Lots of red.
  — This is big work. The paint goes all the way from here to there.
  — This clay looks so smooth and thin now.
  — Did you know that you're the only person in the world who would do this just like you did?

- Avoid *evaluative responses*. Evaluative responses shift the child's focus from his or her work to your praise. In a Godly Play classroom, we want to allow children the freedom to work on what matters most to them, not for the reward of our praise. *Examples of evaluative responses:*
  — You're a wonderful painter.
  — This is a great picture.
  — I'm so pleased with what you did.

- Choose *empowering responses*, which emphasize each child's ability to make choices, solve problems and articulate needs. In a Godly Play classroom, a frequently heard phrase is, "That's the way. You can do this." We encourage children to choose their own work, get the materials out carefully and clean up their work areas when they are done. When a child spills something, respond with, "That's no problem. Do you know where the cleanup supplies are kept?" If a child needs help, show where the supplies are kept or how to wring out a sponge. When helping, the aim is to restore ownership of the problem or situation to the child as soon as possible.

- Stay alert to the children's *needs* during work and cleanup time. The door person's role is especially important as children get out their work. By staying alert to the children's choices in the circle, the door person can know when to help a new child learn the routine for using clay, when a child might need help moving the desert box or when a child might need support in putting material away or cleaning up after painting.

WORKING WITH OLDER CHILDREN

Working with older children opens up new possibilities for the Godly Play teacher. As children reach the ages of 9-12, they are ready for more "languaged" responses and explorations at their new stage of cognitive development.

Teachers can help meet the needs of older children by gradually giving them more of the responsibilities of the room: checking attendance, leading prayers, tending the lights, reading scripture, etc. Spend more time on the community-building as you build the circle. Encourage them to share news from their week before you begin the day's lesson.

At this age, teachers can choose stories and presentations with more layers of language: synthesis stories (such as the Books of the Bible or the Holy Trinity), stories that need reading skills (such as the parable games or the "I am" sayings), side-by-side stories or parables, and stories that work more directly with symbols, such as using the basket of crosses or letting children make their own crosses. You can present an object box lesson, and then encourage the children to create their own object boxes. Children can also make their own parable boxes and other materials.

Use object boxes to present a specific person or symbol. On page 22 in Chapter 2, you can read about making an object box for yourself, as a practice exercise. In *The Complete Guide to Godly Play, Volume 4*, you can find an object box presentation about crosses. Especially when working with older children, you may want to enrich your presentations by making object boxes about biblical figures or saints or heroes.

For example, if you wanted to make an object box for the prophet Miriam, tell how she risked her life to watch over baby Moses. When Pharaoh's daughter found the baby, you can tell about Miriam's brave cunning in offering to find a nurse. Miriam brought back Moses' own mother to nurse the baby! You'll especially want to tell how, when God's People passed safely through the waters, "Miriam led the dancing!"

After collecting the stories, you choose an underlay and objects to place on the underlay. For Miriam, you might choose a blue felt underlay as a reminder of the water that plays an important part in Miriam's stories. For symbols, you might choose a small basket as a reminder of the basket in which baby Moses was placed and a tambourine to symbolize the dances that Miriam led. (If I say any more about this example, it will become my object box and not yours.)

When you tell an object box story, you can roll out the underlay, a bit at a time, from right to left, so that the children will "read" the story from left to right. In the same direction, lay out one symbol at a time to guide your storytelling.

The wondering process can be more drawn out at this age, and teachers can be more challenging in their questions. For example, in telling the story of The Ten Best Ways, teachers can encourage children to ponder more deeply the complexity of the commandments: "How can we keep the commandment 'Do not kill' and stay alive? Anything that grows is alive, from chickens and cows, to carrots and lettuce."

Responses, too, can be more sophisticated at this age level. Some children will now want to read resource books or explore a story through maps. Some children will now want to write during their response time. They are more likely to want to work on sustained projects that take several weeks and can use more sophisticated art materials and processes, such as an intricate tiling project or carefully layered collage. Cooperative projects are now possible, too: banners, murals, models, etc.

REFLECTING: SACRED SPACE AND GODLY PLAY

This reflection exercise works best when you can use the questions as you visit the sacred space of a church and a Godly Play classroom. First sit quietly in the church for at least ten minutes. Then answer the reflection questions below.

Next sit quietly in a Godly Play classroom for ten minutes. Again, answer the same reflection questions. This will give you a kind of interplay between the church and the Godly Play environment for you to ponder. (This is similar to what we mean by a "side-by-side" presentation in Godly Play.)

Reflection Questions:

• I wonder where the threshhold is? What happens to me when I step across this line?

....

....

....

....

....

• I wonder where the central focus of the space is? Does it show what this place is for? How?

....

....

....

....

....

....

• I wonder where the images of the sacred stories are?

....

....

....

....

....

• I wonder where the images of the parables are?

....
....
....
....
....

• I wonder where the symbols for liturgical action are?

....
....
....
....
....

• I wonder what the differences are in the way sacred stories, parables and liturgical action are located in these environments?

....
....
....
....
....

• I wonder where the silence materials are? What images show silence? What helps create and support silence? What is this kind of silence about?

....
....
....
....
....
....

CHAPTER 5

GODLY PLAY SPOKEN HERE

STORYTELLING AS A HEALING ART

The room was very quiet. The lights were low, and the six women leaning back in comfortable chairs, sipping coffee, did not have much to say about the parable spread out before them on a low, glass table. It was before eight o'clock in the morning, and I had just finished telling the Good Shepherd to a group of hospice home-health workers.

As the pause lengthened...and lengthened...I began to feel a little edgy. True, I had suggested that their wondering about the parable might be silent, and internal, and go on long after the story ended. But maybe, I thought, they just don't get it. Maybe they are annoyed with this delay in getting on with their demanding work.

Then the quiet got comfortable, like an old, friendly dog that just wants to sit close to someone who loves it. Finally, there were sighs, and these women—who were about to drive many miles through suburban congestion to far-flung assignments, to perform the dirtiest work of health care—began to talk about how relaxed they felt. Before even approaching the content of the parable, they simply basked in appreciation of a quiet place, a soothing voice and the invitation to be still—to be cared for.

"Maybe I didn't get it," said one of them, who clearly did. "But I saw myself as the shepherd, the caregiver." That launched a deep discussion of the parable and the images that had come to them during the telling. One discovered that her work was to care for the "shell," the body—her interpretation of the sheepfold—and to help the soul make the transition through the open gate. Another, the busy chaplain who had gathered these caregivers, had found herself in a moment of ease, lying in a green meadow at night, looking up at the stars. For someone else, the dark places were caves, which she found comforting and mysterious, as well as dangerous.

Much more went unsaid. After all, these women are masters of the "unspoken lesson." As I said to them in my brief introduction, Godly Play involves both a spoken and an unspoken lesson, and I was not going to teach them about the unspoken lesson. They lived it every day, and I hoped that I could learn from them.

I left the chaplain with a miniversion of the parable, which she and the home-health workers were eager to pass around. I have had the privilege of using the Good Shepherd parable with two hospice patients in my own work, and found it opened doors to memories and feelings that mere words could not. After the first telling, to a woman named Vicki, I sat with the packed-up gold box on my lap. "What did you call that box again?" Vicki asked. A parable, I replied. "I have another name for it," she told me, her eyes glistening. "I call it the box of love."

—Rosemary Beales, Godly Play trainer

In Chapter 4, I outlined how to do Godly Play in its most frequent setting: the religious education classroom. However, Godly Play is more than a Sunday school program. As a way of offering people the language of God's people, it finds a home in many settings. In this chapter, I'll explore some of the ways that Godly Play is spoken outside of the religious education classroom, from pediatric-hospital beds to inner-city streets.

We could call these settings "special situations." A special situation can be as ordinary as visiting your grandmother, and finding a child visiting her at the same time. What can make this a special situation? You can. When you pay loving attention to a child in *any* situation, the event becomes special.

Let's explore some examples of children in special situations:

• Perhaps you are visiting a friend whose parent has died. This is one of the most potent losses that can take place in a child's life. At the time you arrive to be with your friend, her four-year-old daughter wanders into the room. What would you do?

• Children experience other losses. What if a parent moves away, as in a divorce? What if the child and the whole family is moving? For a child, these losses are not trivial disruptions. They represent the destruction of the world the child has come to rely on. How is a child to put that into words? How can the child ask you for help? Because finding the words can be so difficult for children, your own alertness to their needs can offer them unexpected comfort.

• Even the loss of a playmate who is moving is difficult for a child. How can the child know where her friend is going? Time is so problematic for the child. How long will it be before the friend leaves? How long will the child be gone?

• Any sudden difference causes a rush of powerful emotions. Suppose a new child is born into the family. While the infant is in the hospital, the child might find the experience novel and interesting. When the new infant comes home, everything changes for the sibling. Almost certainly, the child will feel left out—perhaps powerless to express those feelings in any constructive way.

• Violent acts create special situations. For the child who is beaten up or bullied, a heightened sense of danger is always in the air. If a child is raped, then shame, uncertainty and confusion are added to the violence.

- What if a child is lonely or depressed? These too are special situations. These children may be overlooked precisely because they are quiet and withdrawn. They do not create a "problem" that draws caregivers' attention.

What happens to children in a special situation? They have *feelings,* and they are entitled to feel these feelings, even—perhaps even especially—feelings of pain. We adults don't like to feel the children's pain. We would rather think of children as naturally happy, not only so that we won't worry about them, but because we are afraid that we might not have what it takes to help a child in pain.

Children play into our misguided evaluations of their strengths and vulnerabilities by doing what they do naturally. They are immature, just as we expect. They may cry with sadness or outrage one moment and then appear happy and at ease the next. They seem not to care about sad events for very long. They forget them easily, we think, especially because that is what we wish. Unfortunately, much of the pain and misunderstanding children experience gets carried in their bodies as much as in their thoughts and feelings.

If we tell a child that someone they love has died, they may cry for a few moments or not at all. They may then demand a soda or cookie and disappear to watch television. Adults sometimes interpret such behavior as proof that children don't care or don't understand. We may find comfort in this explanation, but the explanation is not accurate.

The child is really expressing as much feeling as he or she dares and then retreating in order to recuperate. This is precisely when we need to make ourselves available to children, at their level and at their pace. For example, a child may appear to be playing unconcernedly in the sandbox several days after her grandmother has died. If we look carefully we may notice that she is repeatedly covering a doll with sand. The familiar and safe medium of play is probably being used to express her thoughts and feelings about her grandmother's death and burial and to explore its reality.

Sometimes we are not alert to the needs of children when we enter a special situation, but as our awareness grows, so do our opportunities to help meet the needs of these children. What children need is someone who is real. In this chapter, I'll explore ways of being present to children in special situations and how Godly Play can help.

PASTORAL CARE IN HOSPITALS

From 1974 to 1984, I worked in the Texas Medical Center. I was associated with the Institute of Religion, Texas Children's Hospital and Baylor College of Medicine; for three years I was associated with Houston Child Guidance Center. My experience in pastoral care grew out of my experience of working with sick children and their families in hospitals, as well as working on teams with mental health professionals to provide therapy for families with suicidal children.

Play therapists have long understood the therapeutic power of play. They help children cope with memories of difficult procedures: receiving injections, being stuck for blood samples, getting stitches, having stitches taken out and seeing stitches fall on the floor. Play therapists know that sick children often don't have the energy or vocabulary to articulate the questions troubling them. "Was that part of me?" They also help children play their way into dealing with the fear of the unknown, such as surgery, by playing with materials to make known what the children previously had no experience of. For example, they might use a doll house surgical suite to prepare for surgery.

In my work, it was the play therapists at Texas Children's Hospital who first understood the difference between play therapy and theological play. They knew they could help children with the fear of the unknown by making it more known, but what if the child's spoken or unspoken question is, "Am I going to die?" There is something very different about that concern and the concern about what surgery or a shot will be like. This is an existential matter. It involves the mystery of the presence of God, so the response needs to be with theological play. A language change is needed from the language of everyday and the hospital to the language of religion with its strange stories and liturgical symbols. The play therapists at the Texas Children's Hospital knew immediately what Godly Play was for, because they spent so much time with children right at the boundary of life and death.

Of course, using concrete materials with children in hospitals, even children in isolation, requires careful consultation with the medical staff. For example, felt and foamcore are hard to disinfect, and could present a danger to children whose immune systems are lowered by chemotherapy. However, more important than the specific materials used is the quality of our presence to a child in a special situation. Once a chaplain at Texas Medical Center told me a story about walking down the hospital hall. Someone asked her to see a child who could not seem to stop crying.

The chaplain had no play bag or parable with her, so she went into the nurses' station. There she got some balls of cotton and tore off a piece of blue paper surrounding the cotton. She found brown paper and tore that into narrow strips. She took off the green scarf around her neck, then went into the room and laid her scarf out as the underlay for the parable of the Good Shepherd. (See *The Complete Guide to Godly Play, Volume 3*.) The child became interested in what was going on, stopped crying and began to make meaning, both with the parable and the presence of the parable's Creator in the parable.

DALLAS CHILDREN'S MEDICAL CENTER

Dallas Children's Medical Center is an accredited center for Clinical Pastoral Education and for teaching the specialty of pediatric pastoral care. Godly Play has been part of their pastoral care and training since 1987.

At the Center, chaplains use tote bags to bring parables and other materials to the children in their beds. (The miniature parable boxes and other miniature Godly Play materials from Godly Play Resources, described in the Appendix, were first made at the request of pastoral care providers who wanted children in bed to be able to use these materials.) The Center presents Godly Play stories and liturgical presentations in several ways: by television, by chaplain visits and by the children's attendance at worship in the hospital chapel, which is also equipped with Godly Play materials.

The director of the program, Ron Somers-Clark, says, "When I came to Dallas Children's Medical Center in 1983, I realized from the beginning that we needed to be more creative in our approach to children. I heard about Jerome Berryman when he was at the cathedral in Houston, and decided I would go down to hear him present a workshop on parables.

"Here was someone using the words *theological play* who had begun to reframe how to address the needs of children in an age-appropriate way. When I went there, he was demonstrating this in classrooms, but he had worked in hospital settings, too. Through Godly Play, we could invite children to interact with us in the face of their pain, their worries and their sense of being out of control.

"We use these stories, first of all, in daily devotions in chapel. We sit down on the floor in the chapel, and an experienced chaplain tells a sacred story. People in their rooms can watch on closed-circuit TV. In the chapel itself, we have small, movable pews, with very comfortable, cushioned seats for children who may be in pain and discomfort. The space is arranged so that we can have devotions in the round, with a circle space in the middle. Our closed-circuit TV camera can zoom right in to focus on the story itself.

"The challenge comes when we take the stories upstairs. We buy big canvas bags from Lands' End that stand up, and monogram the word *chaplain* on the side. Chaplains fill the bags with parable boxes and art supplies, such as coloring sheets and crayons. We want to be creative in our child-centered approach to pastoral care, so the mystery begins with the bag itself. 'I see you're looking at my bag up here. I've got some neat stuff. Do you want to look?' Then, with a child whose parents are open to this, maybe on a presurgical visit, we can say, 'While we're waiting, would you like to hear a story?'

"One of my more dramatic memories of a Godly Play story was about a twelve-year-old girl whose primary caretaker was her grandma. She was in the hematology oncology ward, for a bone marrow transplant, and she wouldn't speak to anyone. No one. As in so many cases, when everything else has been tried, they called the chaplain, Mark. Mark went up, greeted her, and spoke about a previous visit. He tried to reestablish this past relationship, but she wouldn't speak to him.

"And so he said, 'You know what I forgot? I am so sorry. I remember that you like our sacred stories. Would you like me to go get one?' No answer. 'I think I will go down and get one. Let's see which one was your favorite?' No answer. He went and got the parable of the Good Shepherd.

"'Let's see. Should I tell this story on the bed or on the floor?' No response. He sat on floor and told the story. When he got to the wondering part, he said, 'I wonder if you can remember any scary places like this, where the sheep were?' And the girl said her first words: 'The tank.' In Texas a tank is a man-made pond. She and her grandmother had gone down fishing and the girl had seen a big catfish. If you've never seen a catfish—well, they scare me! Those were her first words, and she continued to talk.

"Well, geez, what's religious or spiritual about that? The nurses on the floor proclaimed, 'This is some kind of miracle'. I agree. I think it is a kind of miracle. To be able to listen or to be present with a child or a parent, and to bring them to voice, to have them speak words, is to connect with their souls and their spirits.

"We also do a values clarification group with older teenagers. Because the stories transcend denominational differences, even faith differences, they honor religious, spiritual and faith boundaries. A favorite story with this group is the parable of The Good Samaritan. We'll ask, 'Who did you like the most in this story? Who do you think you might identify with most in this story?' Some will answer, 'Maybe I'm like one of the people who passed by on the other side', or even, 'Maybe I'm like the robber!' And some of them say, 'What the Good Samaritan did? This is the way I would like to be more...'

"We work with eating disorder groups and are even developing ministries for waiting areas, where lay volunteers can go into these bus-station-like settings and be with families and children. When there aren't answers, these stories help people find a way to be in the midst of the suffering with some hope. That's the real challenge in pastoral care. 'I've been a good parent, I don't smoke, I eat right...how could my child be born with this?' We hear this all the time.

"Godly Play offers a gentle response. The stories and the chapel services are uniquely oriented to the child, yet families know they're being cared for as well. They can see that there's something unique and special in this place. It's an age-appropriate way of communicating hope and presence, so that a child can know, 'I am not alone. I have ultimate value'."

INTERNATIONAL GODLY PLAY

Where else does Godly Play find a home? Wherever people want to create meaning about life and death with the language of God's People. Dr. Courtney Cowart presented Godly Play at a meeting at Canterbury Cathedral in England and found special interest from the African Episcopal bishops, restless from being treated so long as colonials by the church. Dr. Cowart could acknowledge how much more they knew about this than we do. Africans are still a storytelling people, and this work can provide a bridge between their religious traditions and ours. One young priest from Africa with whom I worked wasn't sure that he *could* be that kind of storyteller yet, because he was young. In his culture, you have to earn the right to be a storyteller, by the wisdom and experience of old age.

We now have Godly Play trainers in the United Kingdom and Australia.

GODLY PLAY IN THE HOME

I often recommend that families take along the Creation materials on a vacation. (See *The Complete Guide to Godly Play, Volume 2*.) On the first day of the vacation you can lay out the first card that shows the light divided from darkness and ask, "I wonder if anyone saw light today?" When the family has finished sharing, you can give thanks to God for the gifts of creation you've enjoyed that day. You can make the family creche more than a Christmas decoration by sharing together the story of the Holy Family and Advent. (See *The Complete Guide to Godly Play, Volume 3*.) The lesson of the Faces (also *Volume 3*) provides something for the family to use around the table during Lent.

Cyndy Bishop, a Godly Play trainer, describes a special Godly Play gift for her family. "My four-year-old daughter Madeleine just received a wonderful gift on the fourth anniversary of her baptism. Her godmother, Susan Mills, lovingly compiled all of the pieces of the Baptism lesson—the felt circles, a Christ candle, a snuffer, a pitcher and bowl, the dove, the oil and the baby—and placed them all in a white container so she could have her very own baptism story. A group of us had visited Father Jambor's classrooms at All Saints in Fort Worth this summer. Susan and I had a favorite room that we decided we would like to recreate in our own homes when we had the resources.

"Madeleine has worked with the Baptism lesson several times now. I supervise when matches are involved! Madeleine told the story to her two-year-old sister, Isabel, who now talks about 'changing the light'. I have tried to get Madeleine to let the baby stay in the container with the other materials but she insists on sleeping with it every night. The day after receiving her gift, she and Susan's daughter Clare, my god-daughter, played at their house. We heard the sink fill up with water and saw

Madeleine walking to the bathroom with one of Clare's dolls behind her back. They proceeded to baptize every doll they could find."

GODLY PLAY IN OTHER RELIGIOUS SETTINGS

Religious education is the most frequent setting for Godly Play in church, of course. The ordinary materials are too small to serve as the focal point for a sermon or liturgy, because people in the congregation can't see the materials. However, occasionally people have found a way to make a liturgical use of Godly Play work by making it *big*.

One California church told the Christmas story by making a giant gold box. As the storyteller told the story, the story came out of the box: people came out from behind the box and moved into place, as living story figures used in the presentation. In Maryland, another church has made giant creation cards. For a bishop's consecration in Delaware, children painted onto huge banners the Faces of Christ (see *The Complete Guide to Godly Play, Volume 4*) and carried them in procession into the church.

This approach to religious education can find expression in other religious traditions, too, though here care must be taken to use the appropriate language and symbols of that tradition. In London, Rabbi Dr. Michael Shire was then director of the Centre for Jewish Education and one of the leaders of Godly Play in England. When I visited the Centre to hold a conference, it was called "Doing Midrash with Jerome." Rabbi Shire's perspective reminds us that the sacred stories of what we call the Old Testament are stories we receive with respect from our Jewish teachers.

What about religious traditions apart from Judaism and Christianity? In volume 91 of *Religious Education* (Winter, 1996) there was an article by John Hull called "A Gift to the Child: A New Pedagogy for Teaching Religion to Young Children." In the article, Hull described a method of teaching various religions in English schools through a hands-on approach, using three-dimensional teaching aids which Dr. Hull and his team called "numens." (I was a consultant for this project.)

They selected their numens by three criteria. First, the objects must be a somewhat self-enclosed entity within the life and faith of a particular religion. Second, the object, such as the elephant Ganesha for the Hindu people or the cross for Christian folk, is charged with a sense of the sacred which draws one toward worship. Third, the object has "gifts" to offer the children, although we cannot know in advance how or in what insights those gifts will manifest themselves to the children.

GODLY PLAY IN THE COMMUNITY

Godly Play teachers have taken stories into all kinds of settings, such as retirement centers, where older people may not say much during the wondering, but show with their faces and eyes how deeply they enter into these stories and parables. We've taken the stories into safe houses and shelters for runaways. In Houston, one setting for runaways was in the Montrose area. I walked into their auditorium with a parable box under one arm and said, "Hi. I've got something strange to show you, if you're interested."

Not many were! One or two came and looked at the box. I started telling the parable of the Good Shepherd anyway. Before I was done, about thirty out of forty teenagers in that room came and gathered around. Perhaps this is less surprising than it sounds. After all, if they weren't really scared and searching, they wouldn't have come into a religious shelter to start with. These kids were very involved in the wondering, because the existential questions of life and death were so close to their skin.

Sometimes Godly Play even takes to the streets. Trainer Laura McGuire helped Beth McNamara, an Episcopal priest at the Church of the Resurrection, plan and carry out a Godly Play ministry that told the stories on the streets of Baltimore. Beth said, "The trick is to find the right spot to tell the stories, and the right medium to get the message out. We were blessed in having a small bit of green space surrounding a library across the street from the church, as well as lots of wall space at church and sidewalk space to put up fliers on the days we were presenting stories. When we tried doing the same program in a much larger park, close to a swimming pool, we had no luck at all, probably because there were no good (or legal!) ways of putting up fliers."

Beth and her helpers loaded up a cart with a Godly Play story, bath towels for the children to sit on, drawing boards with paper attached, boxes of juice and markers. They marched out of their church and to the green and grassy space, so reminiscent of the gospel description of where Jesus shared bread and fish with thousands of people. Soon dozens of children had joined the circle to share story, art and a feast in this unusual Godly Play space.

GODLY PLAY WITH OLDER PEOPLE

My oldest Godly Play participants were residents of the Deerfield Retirement Community in Asheville, North Carolina. They were in their 70s, 80s and 90s. To see for yourself what happened, order a video of this event from the Episcopal Diocese of Western North Carolina (828-669-2921).

WHY IT MATTERS

Suzi Robertson, who is now parish educator at Trinity Episcopal Church in Galveston, Texas, and a Godly Play trainer, tells a story that perhaps best illustrates why taking Godly Play into "special situations" can make a difference.

"I've known Jerome for many years. I was intrigued by his work, because Godly Play helps children to develop their theology, *not* by telling them the way things are but by asking them questions. It elicits reflective thinking and spontaneous acts of meaning.

"At Christ Church Cathedral, I became involved with a young and unique family when the little boy's mother called me to ask me if Brandon could be baptized. I was the person at the cathedral who dealt with all the baptisms, and as in most places, before you present a child, parents are expected to attend an orientation class.

"The father said that was not one of their plans. I described our full process and he said, 'Well, we don't have time to do all that because Brandon has cancer and he's really, really sick.' I invited the two parents to come and talk to me, while Brandon was at school.

"During our conversation, the mother was continually paged as Brandon struggled through his day at school. I could see how traumatic things had become for them and I said, 'I'll cut a deal with you. This is early November. We will baptize him on December 13, during our evening service. But at least one of you needs to become a member here, and Brandon needs to come to Sunday school every Sunday until he is baptized.

"They brought Brandon in all wrapped up, so sick that he couldn't walk. When they came to pick him up he asked, 'Can I come back here next week?' He kept coming and was baptized in December. Over Christmas break, the family traveled to visit relatives. Brandon had a stroke and was airlifted back to the hospital. On Epiphany his mother called me to say that Brandon wanted to see me. He didn't want to go back to school but he did want to come back to Sunday school.

"So the Sunday after Epiphany, Brandon was in Sunday school, when the parable of the Good Shepherd was being told. After the wondering, the teacher asked the children if they had any wondering questions of their own. Brandon said, 'I have two. If one of the sheep gets lost and the Good Shepherd can't find him, but is really sad, is the Good Shepherd still with him? And if one of the sheep gets so sick that he dies is the Good Shepherd sad and still with him?'

"Someone answered, 'The Good Shepherd is with you no matter what'.

"I learned two things from this experience. Brandon hadn't been raised in a religious tradition, so he didn't even necessarily know that the Good Shepherd is Jesus, but he *met* Jesus, through the story, even though he didn't know the shepherd's name. He learned that he didn't have to die by himself, whenever it came time for him to die.

"I also learned that Godly Play is a form of discipleship for children, because if I did not have a way to invite Brandon to enter into this children's community, he would have been baptized but never seen again. And for *him*, baptism would have been nothing but a little water sprinkled on him."

REFLECTING:
SPECIAL SETTINGS FOR GODLY PLAY

Godly Play seems to go where it is needed, but now it is time for you to reflect on your own experiences. Reflect on situations where you are already present: home, church, work, ministry. You can also reflect on places where you feel called to be present:

• How do you feel your situation presents a special challenge?

....

....

....

....

....

....

• What strengths does Godly Play offer to your particular work?

....

....

....

....

....

• How could you adapt Godly Play procedures and materials to meet these challenges?

....

....

....

....

....

CHAPTER 6

ENTERING THE TRADITION*

COMING TO OUR OWN CONCLUSIONS

I was doing the Circle of the Church Year presentation with a group of five- to ten-year-olds. In the wondering, I teased them by saying, "We've got so many of these little pieces, it would be simpler to take some away. What could we just take away?"

They automatically wondered about the endless green season going on too long, but I pushed them further—sensing, I suppose, that they were being a bit too pious and unplayful? I picked out the pieces for the three great festivals and said, "What about one of these, Christmas, Easter, Pentecost? Let's leave one of these out."

Then the group really came to life! Spontaneously they formed three "camps," one to defend the importance of Christmas, one to defend Easter and a third to defend Pentecost. No one mentioned Christmas presents or Easter eggs! They argued between themselves on theological grounds, coming finally to their own conclusion that each festival depended on the others for its full meaning.

—Rebecca Nye, Godly Play trainer

Godly Play is my way of entering the Montessori tradition of religious education with children. That tradition goes back to Maria Montessori herself, and has given birth to many variations. Of course, I'm committed to my own approach, but I want to stress again: I'm not saying everyone should do Godly Play. I'm just describing what I do and trying to explain why. As you enter into this tradition of religious education yourself, you may find yourself wondering how to choose which approaches to the tradition work best for you. My suggestion, for me and for all of us who want to experiment within the Montessori tradition, is to watch the children and see what happens. Perhaps another variation will arise for the next generation that incorporates the strengths of all that has come before.

The tradition as it stands now consists of four generations. Maria Montessori represents the first generation, and her students, particularly E. M. Standing, represent the second. The third generation is represented by Sofia Cavalletti, whose work has given new impetus to the Montessori tradition of religious education. I regard myself and others as members of the fourth generation, those who want to build on the work of Montessori, Standing and Cavalletti. Let's begin by examining expressions of the *fourth* generation in North America.

*Funding for researching this chapter was generously provided by the Lily Endowment.

THE FOURTH GENERATION: A PERSONAL VIEW OF A GROWING AND DIVERSE MOVEMENT

The influence of Montessori religious education is spreading throughout the world. This is especially due to the work of Sofia Cavalletti who began in 1954 in Rome to teach children the Christian way, using the Montessori method. Her teaching began almost at once to attract wide and enthusiastic attention in Italy and other countries.

In 1963 Cavalletti founded the Maria Montessori Association for the Religious Formation of the Child, which included people all over the world. Her latest book, *The Religious Potential Between 6-12 Years: A Description of an Experience*, published in 1996 and not yet translated into English, includes a list of nations to which this organization has spread: Canada, United States, Mexico, Columbia, Paraguay, Uruguay, Argentina, Italy, Germany, Austria, Croatia, Poland, Chad, Tanzania, Japan and Australia. Children from all sorts of social backgrounds from the upper classes to the poorest of the poor as well as children from the cities to farms have been involved.

The variety of forms this movement has taken in North America is especially interesting for four reasons:
• Much of this interest has been a grass roots, bottom-up transformation of Christian education values and vision.
• This work has attracted people across many different denominational lines, from Roman Catholics to the Free Church tradition.
• Within denominational lines a wide variety of religious orientations such as evangelical, charismatic, high church, low church, liberal, conservative and others have become involved.
• At a time when many assume that volunteers are not interested in taking the time to prepare themselves for religious education or taking an interest in children's long-term growth, this movement, which requires much work and dedication, continues to spread.

Six major variations of the Montessori approach to religious education are especially prominent in North America. Since I have been involved in each of these approaches, to some degree, they are also the variations I know best. The six approaches are:
• The Catechesis of the Good Shepherd
• Young Children and Worship
• Jubilee
• Augsburg Youth and Family Ministry
• the Pastoral Care Department of Children's Medical Center of Dallas (described in Chapter 5)
• Godly Play

CATECHESIS OF THE GOOD SHEPHERD

The Catechesis of the Good Shepherd is the organization in the United States that provides a direct link today through the work of Sofia Cavalletti to the tradition of Montessori religious education. By the time *The Religious Potential of the Child* was published in English by Paulist Press in 1983, the Good Shepherd had become the central image for Cavalletti's approach. The centrality of the Good Shepherd as a way to introduce children to Jesus and to Holy Communion is one of Cavalletti's most important discoveries.

The spread of Cavalletti's work to North America roughly parallels my own discovery of this approach, so I will become somewhat more autobiographical from this point on, telling the part of the story I was directly involved in.

In 1971 I was studying to become a Montessori teacher at The Center for Advanced Montessori Studies in Bergamo, Italy, a city northeast of Milan where the Alps begin. My intuition had told me that this might be a superb way to teach religious education, so I was exploring that possibility in a systematic way while I took the general course.

Imagine my surprise and delight when Sofia Cavalletti came to Bergamo in the winter to give a lecture and demonstrate some of her three-dimensional teaching materials. When our family returned to the United States, traveling through Rome to visit her again, I began at once to experiment with this approach in Cleveland and then in Houston in both schools and churches.

Although I had taken the general Montessori course in Italy and was an experienced Montessori teacher, I still had not been able to study with Cavalletti at her Center in Rome, so in 1978 I brought her to Houston. She presented an international course which took place June 26 – July 21, 1978 at St. Mary's Seminary with Spanish translation. People attended from Italy and Canada, but most came from the United States and Mexico. They were able to receive continuing education, college or graduate credit through the University of St. Thomas in Houston.

This Course was given under the name of the Institute of Religion in the Texas Medical Center where I was a professor of theology and ministry. This was, I believe, the third time Sofia had come to North America, previously visiting Minneapolis and Toronto to give courses. The course in Minneapolis was given in 1975. The organization of The Catechesis of the Good Shepherd soon took place, and by 1996 it had grown to 412 members, producing a newsletter as well as an extensive formation network to provide teacher training.

I revisited my own training with Cavalletti by taking the course again when it was given in the Houston area in 1993. It was a splendid opportunity to catch up with old friends, as well as to see how the training (and I) had evolved.

One major difference between the 1978 and the 1993 courses was that Cavalletti was not present in 1993. Her work, however, was well-represented by many of her most experienced students.

By 1993 it was clear that I could no longer be said to be presenting Cavalletti's curriculum in my workshops. That was now the responsibility of the Catechesis of the Good Shepherd organization. What I was doing was something different although still within the larger tradition of Montessori religious education and still heavily influenced by my own interpretation of Cavalletti's work.

Although my relationship with Catechesis of the Good Shepherd could be viewed as either a contribution or a defection, all I can describe is my own perception of my experience. Sofia Cavalletti is a friend, a generous mentor and colleague. She once told me that I am "like a good Montessori child," which means that I need to think things through for myself and use my own experience with the children and my own creativity to know what is true. My "contributions" may have moved me in some different directions from Sofia's work, but, it seems to me, this probing and testing has helped not only to spread but also to deepen the Montessori tradition of religious education in this country.

A major step in spreading this approach to the general community of scholars was taken on November 11, 1977, when I presented a paper at the Religious Education Association meeting in St. Louis called "Montessori, The Parables and Human Faith," which was revised and published in *Religious Education* in 1979 as "Being in Parables with Children." I also proposed that Sofia Cavalletti be a keynote speaker at the next Religious Education Association meeting in Toronto. She was invited, but was not able to come.

On November 23, 1979, I took Cavalletti's place in Toronto with David Elkind to address the plenary session of this international group. The talk was organized around a series of slides of children working in my center in Houston at the Institute of Religion. The slides included children's art responses to presentations, some of which were like Cavalletti's and some of which I had developed. What I actually said, however, is only a blur, because the first slides jammed in the projector!

Cavalletti was supportive of these explorations. She invited me to present some of my new work with children at a conference in Mexico City on July 6, 1981, during a much longer course she was giving there. This time the slide projector worked beautifully! I also read a paper in Rome on April 22, 1982, at an occasion organized by the Maria Montessori Association for the Religious Formation of the Child which also showed some of my experimentation with particular lessons and with the whole learning environment and process.

We have continued to correspond, and we used to visit back and forth. She would stop in Houston on her way to Mexico, and sometimes our whole family or my wife,

Thea Berryman, and I would visit in Rome. My last visit of more than a few days, supported by the Lilly Endowment, came in 1991. In the same year, Cavalletti graciously reviewed my book *Godly Play* in *Vita dell'Infanzia*, a monthly magazine devoted to a wide range of matters related to Montessori education. In 1997 I was also present at an international conference and celebration of the work of Sofia Cavalletti and Gianna Gobbi held September 7-12 in Assisi.

Another major step toward making Cavalletti's work known in North America was taken in 1982. I urged Jean Marie Hiesberger, then an editor at Paulist Press, to publish Cavalletti's *The Religious Potential of the Child*. At the editor's suggestion I wrote the Introduction to the first English edition, which was published in 1983, as mentioned above.

By this time the Association was active in the United States and was organizing national courses. The first part of the course about children from three to six years of age had been given in Washington in 1982. When *The Religious Potential of the Child* went out of print, the organization printed it privately with a new introduction to help with the teaching of their courses and for the general public to be introduced to Cavalletti's work.

The success of the organization of The Catechesis of the Good Shepherd has allowed me to be more free with my experiments, now that I know that Cavalletti's work is being faithfully presented in this country. I have called what I do "Godly Play" to highlight the quality of the relationships involved. This stresses the importance of engaging the creative process through play to be open to the complex relationship we can enjoy with the Holy Trinity.

YOUNG CHILDREN AND WORSHIP

The publication of *Young Children and Worship*, which I jointly authored with Sonja Stewart, has also had a great deal to do with the growth of interest in Montessori religious education, because by 2002 it had sold over 40,000 copies. Even if these readers are merely thinking about whether or not they want to incorporate some of this approach into their natural teaching style, such a large readership adds to the Montessori religious education conversation.

The book began when Sonja Stewart came to Houston in 1985 with three of her graduate students to take one of the workshops I was offering then at Christ Church Cathedral. The next year I went to Western Seminary in Holland, Michigan, where she is Professor of Christian Education, and presented a workshop there. *Young Children and Worship* was one result of these visits.

A second outcome of these visits was that Professor Stewart began to offer her own fine, weeklong workshops, using the version of the Montessori approach to religious education contained in *Young Children*. A related program called "Young Children and Worship" has been approved for use by the Reformed Church of America, the Christian Reformed Church, and the Presbyterian Church of Canada. Willa Brown is the Associate for Children's Ministry for the Reformed Church of America and directs a team of teacher-trainers whom I have helped train from her denominational office in Grand Rapids, Michigan. I will again work with their trainers in 2003.

JUBILEE: GOD'S GOOD NEWS

Another denominational resource inspired by the Montessori tradition of religious education is called *Jubilee*. The founder and former executive director of this project, Rosella Wiens Regier, came to Houston as did many others of her committee to look at our eight classrooms at Christ Church Cathedral and to enjoy the workshops I gave there three times a year. In addition, Regier was influenced by meeting Sonja Stewart, as well as by the work of Maria Harris and the writing of Mary Elizabeth Moore and Walter Bruggeman. All these resources have influenced the *Jubilee* curriculum.

Jubilee was created by six denominations representing the Anabaptist part of the Christian family. These denominations are: Brethern in Christ Church, Church of the Brethern, Friends United Meeting, General Conference Mennonite Church, Mennonite Brethren and the Mennonite Church. They have produced training videos, curriculum materials and hands-on teaching figures. Some of their wooden teaching materials are made by people in Central America and furnished to teachers in this country through their missions.

AUGSBURG YOUTH AND FAMILY INSTITUTE

Another center of activity using the Montessori tradition of religious education is the Augsburg Youth and Family Institute in Minneapolis. The Institute is on the campus of Augsburg College and was founded by Merton Strommen. He is the link between the well-known Search Institute devoted to empirical research and Augsburg Youth and Family Institute. Search Institute helps from time to time with the empirical studies that undergird the Institute's work.

Merton Strommen articulated four imperatives of youth and family ministry. In Strommen's view, such ministry is a system that involves:
• the family
• Christian education
• attention to the Christian youth subculture
• a congregational sense of family

Through these partnerships, religious education in the home can be nourished and supported by congregations. This is important, because research shows that the most important religious education takes place at home, whether parents are intentional about this or not.

This group has developed a program to help churches and families work together to recenter religious education in the home. At its core you will find the Montessori approach, including a section I authored about Godly Play in the home.

CHILDREN'S MEDICAL CENTER OF DALLAS

The place I know of in North America where the use of Godly Play is most developed for pastoral care in hospitals is Dallas Children's Medical Center. In Chapter 5, I discuss more fully this accredited center for Clinical Pastoral Education and for teaching the specialty of pediatric pastoral care.

GODLY PLAY

In addition to my Montessori training in Italy and my training with Cavalletti and others in her approach to the tradition of Montessori religious education, my theological education was at Princeton Theological Seminary (M. Div., 1962; D. Min., 1996). I am an Episcopal priest and, for a decade, was Canon Educator at Christ Church Cathedral in downtown Houston.

As more people joined the Montessori tradition of religious education through Godly Play, talk about forming an organization also increased. Since I had been introduced to the tradition through Sofia Cavalletti and within the context of my own Montessori training, I did not, at first, feel this need as keenly as others. Nonetheless the Center for the Theology of Childhood was incorporated on December 22, 1997, and has grown into an organization that serves not only its original purpose of researching Godly Play and the theology of childhood, but also to develop and nourish a network of committed Godly Play trainers, teachers and supporters.

In addition, Godly Play Resources, a separate organization based in Kansas, exists to help people provide the many materials used to teach in this way. For those who have the time and talent to do it, making your own materials is always best. In many churches, talented crafts people find a joyful way to support the religious education program by making materials. However, many other people find the provision of materials a real obstacle in beginning to teach this way. They need help!

My brother Tom Berryman and I set up a small corporation in Ashland, Kansas on February 7, 1994, to make many of the educational aids needed in various price ranges, to develop new teaching materials, and to help in other ways. Ashland is the small community in southwestern Kansas where our family settled in the latter part of the 19th century and where my brother still lives. The people who make these beautiful materials are men and women engaged in farming, ranching, carpentry, raising families, teaching school, working for pipeline companies and in other activities. Their involvement in the Godly Play movement is something they do in their spare time as a contribution to the spirituality of children.

Godly Play, then, is a resource for those wishing to explore the Montessori approach to religious education and how it can be used in churches, in schools, in pastoral care settings such as hospitals or therapy, or at home with families. It is a distinct voice in this grand conversation of many generations, seeking to know where God is leading us to better understand what is best to help children be open to God in the complexity and simplicity of the Holy Trinity and to know the powerful language of revelation we have inherited through the Christian tradition.

CONCLUSION

Many people, including myself, have been confused by the variety of forms the Montessori tradition of religious education has taken in North America. You will be grateful to know that I have not even mentioned all the variations I am aware of, only the major ones! This presentation, like my own Montessori practice, is a personal one. I share it with you to give you perspective on the variety that Montessori religious education in North America has developed. Equipped with this perspective and using it to reflect on your own experience, you will be better able to find your own place in this rich and diverse conversation. There is plenty of joyful work (play) for all of us!

Of course, you will need to remain in tune with your own natural teaching style. Of course, you will be constrained by your denominational and local setting. Of course, there will be limits as to money, talent and time. What should not limit you is the richness the Montessori tradition of religious education provides for your own ministry.

A HISTORY OF THE TRADITION

THE FIRST GENERATION: MARIA MONTESSORI

Maria Montessori (1870–1952) was the first woman to earn a medical degree from the University of Rome (1896). This remarkable woman opened her first school in 1907. Today she is widely known as an educator, but her deep interest in religious education has been overlooked by both the religious education community and by most modern Montessori educators.

Montessori was a complex, strong, creative and very religious human being. In 1910, when she was about forty years old, she took her name off the list of practicing physicians in Rome and committed herself completely to education, advocacy for children and religious education.

Misunderstanding Montessori is easy both because of her complexity and because of the broad range of practice in the schools that use her name. More importantly, scholars who comment on her work often seem uninformed by *direct* training or *experience* with her method.[31] What is not often realized is that Montessori teachers are taught primarily by an oral tradition of practice and supervision rather than by books about her or by her.

One scholar is an exception: Jean Piaget. He attended the 1934 International Congress held in Rome just before Montessori education was banned in Italy. He also served for many years as the President of the Swiss Montessori Society.

One of the misunderstandings about Montessori is that there was or is some kind of conflict between Piaget's work and her own. David Elkind has challenged this view, pointing out that Piaget's training in biology and Montessori's training as a physician gave them both a biological view of human growth and development.[32] Both were fascinated by the developmental structures of human beings rather than individual differences among children. Neither minimized the importance of individual differences, but they argued that an understanding of normal development is necessary for a full understanding of such differences. Further, Montessori and Piaget both had what Elkind called "a genius for empathy with the child." Their observations had the "solid ring of truth."

The divergences between Piaget and Montessori are more like a division of labor than a conflict. Piaget wanted to understand the nature and origin of knowledge, so his primary focus was on the area of logic and epistemology. Montessori was also interested in this, but her primary interest was the creation of developmentally appropriate educational environments, materials and methods.

Piaget studied children's thinking and wrote about his experiments and theory. Montessori traveled around the world building schools, training teachers, developing her method and advocating for the rights and needs of children, including religious education.

MONTESSORI AND RELIGION

Montessori once told her close coworker, Anna Maccheroni that:

> Many who haven't understood me think that I'm a sentimental romantic who dreams only of seeing children, of kissing them, of telling them fairy tales, that I want to visit schools to watch them, to cuddle them and give them caramels. They weary me! I am a rigorous scientific investigator, not a literary idealist like Rosseau. I seek to discover the man in the child, to see in him the true human spirit, the design of the Creator: the scientific and religious truth. It is to this end that I apply my method of study, which respects human nature. I don't need to teach anything to children: it is they who, placed in a favorable environment, teach me, reveal to me spiritual secrets as long as their souls have not been deformed.[33]

Some took Montessori's statements to mean that she did not believe in the doctrine of original sin, but she addressed that issue directly in a lecture given in 1948 at the Assumption Convent, Kensington Square, London:

> I see it—this Original Sin—who would not see a thing so evident? In the depths of the human soul is the possibility of continuous decadence, from *alza in balza* [*sic*]. In fact, there are innate tendencies in man's soul which lead to maladies of the spirit sometimes even unknown to ourselves, just as the germs of disease may work silently, and unknown. This is the death of the spirit which brings insensibility with it. These tendencies come from the soul itself and not from the environment.[34]

In 1922 Montessori was fifty-two years old. Her school in Barcelona was what she had dreamed of. It had shaded walks, a meadow, pools for fish, cages for pets, and lots of lovely light and space indoors. She also had an appropriate religious environment for the children. Artists had been hired to make the school chapel the most beautiful space on the campus.

The children experienced worship and instruction about the sacraments from a special priest in a chapel with child-scaled furnishings. Montessori also created sensorial materials about the liturgy and sacred history. In addition children prepared for their first communion by harvesting the wheat, baking the bread and marking the hosts for the celebration. Commenting on the Barcelona experiment she wrote, "The Montessori Method was furnished with a long-sought opportunity of penetrating deeper into the life of the child's soul, and of thus fulfilling its true educational mission."[35]

Montessori discovered that preschool children did most of their learning through the senses in an unconscious, playful way. She termed this play the "work" of the child, because the child was building the structures of cognition that would be used directly and consciously during the next period of development during the elementary school years. This is as true for religious education as it is for general education.

The role of the imagination for child development was of special importance to her. Late in life Montessori wrote, "The child's mind between three and six can not only see by intelligence the relations between things, but it has the higher power still of mentally imagining those things that are not directly visible."[36]

Her view of the imagination's importance is often misunderstood because of quotes, generally read out of context, about fantasy. She knew that adults sometimes used imaginary creatures to threaten children, taking advantage of children's credulity and trust. At other times adults affirm mistakes of children, because they think the children's errors are cute. Both kinds of response show a lack of respect for children, for reality and for the imagination's operations on reality. She vigorously attacked such lapses in adults' respect and appreciation of children!

Montessori also said, "Yet, when all are agreed that the child loves to imagine, why do we give him only fairy tales and toys on which to practice this gift? We often forget that imagination is a force for the discovery of truth. The mind is not a passive thing, but a devouring flame, never in repose, always in action."[37]

In *To Educate the Human Potential*, Montessori wrote that the functions of the mind should not be separated for conscious skill building.[38] Instead, the whole child should be put in touch with the entire "Cosmic Plan" in a way that strikes the child's imagination. That book shows Montessori, the storyteller, at work, and leaves no doubt that with her in a classroom all the children would be drawn into the creative process and find affirmation.

Toward the end of her life Montessori tried again to state the basis of her educational methods:

> I would like to say a word about this reality, and also about the sayings of the poets and the prophets. This force that we call love is the greatest energy of the universe. But I am using an inadequate expression, for it is more than an energy: it is creation itself. I should put it better if I were to say: "God is love."[39]

Montessori asked to be buried where she fell, a citizen of the world and an advocate for the world's children. You will find her final resting place at Noordwijk in The Netherlands, but her legacy continues, including a powerful way to approach religious education today.

THE SECOND GENERATION: E. M. STANDING

E. M. Standing (1887–1967) is especially important for understanding the Montessori tradition of religious education, because of his interpretations of Montessori's work to the English-speaking world and his special interest in her approach to religious education.

Edwin Mortimer Standing was born on September 18, 1887, in Tananarive, Madagascar. He was called "Ted," and grew up in a Quaker missionary family. When Ted was about six years old he went to England for his schooling. Ted was educated in Quaker schools and received his university training at the University of Leeds, from which he graduated about 1909 with a B. Sc. in biology. He earned his Diploma in Education at Cambridge University the next year and then went to Germany for a brief period to study at the University of Freiburg.

Ted Standing, like many others, found his vocation when he met Dr. Maria Montessori. They met in 1921, probably at her London Course. She helped him arrange a year in India (1921–1922) as the teacher of the many children of the Sarabhai family. When he returned to Europe, he took her training course again, probably in Barcelona, and made himself useful in the movement from then on.

Ted wrote that this "spiritual technique" was "something akin to a religious conversion..." Certainly, it was a new way of seeing children: their "sensitive periods," their natural dignity, the significance of their "spontaneous" activities, the wider and more thorough understanding of their needs and "planes of development," and the appreciation of the child as the creator of the adult. It was also a new way of seeing adults. Montessori suggested that working with children in this way can also put us more deeply in touch with the Creator. Some found this to be true, and Ted Standing was one of them.

E. M. STANDING AS MONTESSORI'S INTERPRETER

E. M. Standing is best known for his biography *Maria Montessori: Her Life and Work*.[40] Montessori wrote to him: "I am not making any comments on the substance of it because here is an apostle who is voicing his own enthusiastic impressions. I have, however, made some minor corrections in matters of 'historical' detail. I am impatient to see the whole book..."[41] She died before it was finished.

Montessori's style mixed psychology, philosophy, anthropology, history, ethics and advocacy for children into a passionate and persuasive statement. Some careful, modern readers like myself have become frustrated by this mixture of what we today see as distinct fields of discourse, each with its own kind of logic and way of validating statements. Standing's publications helped unmix her style. He also pulled together her main ideas, which she worked out in a long list of publications over many years. Her bibliography fills a book of its own, some eighty-seven pages long.[42]

In his biography of Montessori, Standing wrote little about her religious education, "striking and original as it is."[43] The subject was beyond the scope of the book. Nevertheless, Christian assumptions are everywhere, especially as the foundation for the "spiritual" training of the teacher.

Standing's books were translated into French, Spanish, Japanese and perhaps other languages, and he loved the role of the writer. He also wrote poetry and short stories as well as articles about education. His shorter writings appeared in the *Atlantic*, *Sower*, *Irish Rosary*, *America*, *Times* (London) and in educational journals. His articles on religious education ranged from one called "Montessori Practice and Thomistic Principle" to another called "The Narrative Method Versus the Catechism."

E. M. Standing's greatest contribution to religious education was his book *The Child in the Church*. It was first published by Montessori in 1922 in Naples as a booklet of around fifty-two pages called *I bambini viventi nella Chiesa (The Children Living in the Church)*. Montessori, then about fifty-two years old and living in Barcelona, was reporting on her first experiments in this field.

Standing expanded Montessori's booklet into a larger version of 191 pages in English in 1929. The latest and most expanded version was published in 1965. By this time it had grown to 224 pages, and included chapters by other major figures of the second and third generations of Montessorians working in religious education. Mother Isabel Eugenia, R.A., M. and F. Lanternier, and Sofia Cavalletti, as well as Standing, were represented.

Mother Isabel Eugenia had been the President of the Catholic Montessori Guild and Principal of the Maria Assumpta Training College in London. This Guild was founded in 1952, the year Montessori died. E. M. Standing, who then called himself "E. Mortimer Standing," was the Chairman.

M. Lanternier had a school in Limoges and then in Rennes, France. He was a former French army officer, and had integrated the liturgical year into the school's life. It culminated in the reliving of Holy Week. Among other innovations, some 200 wooden figures were moved about amid the buildings and streets of a model Jerusalem to help tell the story.

Sofia Cavalletti also contributed a chapter. In 1954 she began in Rome to use Montessori's approach to religious education, and today her Catechetical Center is the leading source of both inspiration and learning about this approach in the world.

STANDING AND MONTESSORI

When Ted Standing first met Montessori in 1921, distressing divisions were beginning to appear among Montessorians in England. The split was between those who felt that Montessori had already said everything that needed to be said about child development and education and those who did not. The Movement was in danger of losing its vital spirit and becoming hardened into a kind of rigid orthodoxy.

In the early 1920s, the battle between the national and the international Montessori organizations in England was so intense that *Punch* could not restrain comment:

> Sing, Muse, the tragic story of the Montessorian split
> And the lurid possibilities arising out of it,
> Revealing how "paedologists," though normally urbane
> May develop, on occasion, quite a first-class fighting strain.[44]

The relationship between Montessori herself and Standing remained one of trust. He was not given to much innovation and not only resisted the bitterness of these conflicts but also avoided the cynicism that can result from a disappointed idealism.

One of the reasons for Standing's fairness and calm may have been that he stayed in contact with children, teaching. Also, Standing had contact directly with Montessori when he needed it. In addition, his travel took him to Rome around 1926 where he lived, working "in collaboration with the Dottoressa." It was probably sometime during 1926 that he was baptized as a Roman Catholic.

A NEW WAY OF LEARNING FOR RELIGIOUS EDUCATION

Standing wrote: "The difficulty in realizing the immense significance of Dr. Montessori's work is that it presents so many different facets, each fascinating in itself, that it is not easy to see the movement as a whole.... For this reason it is fatally easy to regard it *spezzato* (as Montessori would say), i.e., broken into separate pieces."[45]

To avoid *spezzato* we will follow the main lines of Standing's summary in the 1929 edition of *The Child in the Church*. When Montessori principles of education are extended "to the study of the Supernatural Order," religious education's key becomes "Liberty in a Prepared Environment."

The "prepared environment" refers to the setting up of a place where the child can be at home in body, mind and spirit. The little tables and chairs, low shelves, pictures hung at eye-level for the child and other such details were designed for the whole child. Why take energy away from the child's development by using it to adjust to an adult environment?

The "Materials for Development" and relationships in this environment are also for the child's integration of body, mind and spirit. Think of a little child polishing a brass model of a chalice and paten. At one level there is the bodily activity of mastering the act of polishing. The next level is polishing the chalice and the paten to contribute to their beauty and the common responsibility for the care of the classroom. Thirdly, there is the level where the child *consciously* ponders the meaning of the presence of the Mystery of God in Holy Communion as the polishing takes place. This approach promotes both development and the integration of body, mind and spirit.

In an environment with nothing to climb on, Standing wrote, you would never notice that monkeys are naturally developed for climbing. In the same way, children do not reveal their true nature until they can function in an appropriate environment. It is then that the "New Child" appears, tending toward order, deep concentration, self-direction and a joy and serenity in learning.

Yet, liberty in such an environment does not mean license to do anything you want or to use the developmental materials in any way you wish. Things are to be used for the purpose they are intended. True liberty is to be able to choose well and then will the chosen activity. Choices are made among constructive alternatives.

A child's mind is not a "sack" to be filled with facts. It is a "dynamic principle" which needs to be approached indirectly for learning. Standing reminds us that learning occurs by personal discovery, not by the imposition of an adult.

Montessori suggested that young children from about three through six or seven years like to use their senses, and children from about six through twelve years prefer the imagination for learning. A child of four years might love to trace his or her finger over a sandpaper letter, but a child of twelve would think that silly.

To not be aware of what Montessori called the "sensitive periods" or periods of "natural interest" is to risk "dropped stitches." The knitting together of knowledge and the person will still take place but the depth and breadth of the "knitting" will not be as great. Montessori's favorite example of this was to note how easily young children learn languages as compared to the difficulty adults have. The sensitive period for learning languages, including religious language, is before six years of age.

Standing was fond of quoting G. K. Chesterton on the imagination: "When we are very young we do not need fairy tales. Mere life is interesting enough."[46] He was always quick to assure his readers that Montessori was not against fairy tales. What she was concerned about was maintaining the connection between the imagination and sensorial reality.

When children can focus on particular developmental materials and carry through their discoveries to completion, a joyful calm takes over. They become ordered in body, mind and spirit. They also move from the concrete to the abstract as they grow. If you ask a child why he or she no longer does sums with a sensorial material like a bead frame, he or she will say, "I can do it quicker without it."

For Montessori, teacher preparation was not just about knowledge and culture but also "the way in which we regard the child."[47] One must be prepared inwardly to avoid being too much occupied with controlling misbehavior. The primary defect Montessori saw in most teachers was a combination of anger and pride.

Respect is usually reserved for the strong, but children are weak. They cannot defend themselves, so there is nothing to restrain adult anger. This is why teachers need humility before this creation of God. If they do not have such humility, teachers can never know the power of God that is present in childhood and childhood play.

THE SPREADING OF MONTESSORI RELIGIOUS EDUCATION

Montessori escaped from Barcelona and the Spanish Civil War on a British warship in 1936. She went to England for the Fifth International Montessori Congress to be held at Lady Margaret Hall, Oxford. Standing by that time was firmly fixed in the close circle of friends that surrounded Montessori and her work. At the Congress he was one of three on the Committee for Press Information, and he may have been employed as a lecturer or a "Conference Tutor." Two-hundred delegates came from nearly every country in Europe as well as from South America and India.

In England, interest in Montessori religious education centered around London. Montessori gave a course on religious education at the request of Mother Isabel Eugenia in 1936 at Assumption College.

Pictures in the 1965 edition of *The Child in the Church* show the children at London's St. Anthony's School working in a well-developed program with materials about the liturgy and sacred history, and with time lines about saints and church leaders. Sister Stephanie, O.S.F., the Headmistress, was also involved in the Catholic Montessori Guild as Honorary Secretary.

In Scotland, a major center for this type of education was established in Glasgow. The Sisters of Notre Dame of Namur had a school at Dowanhill. In addition to having some 300 young children in Montessori classes, they had a high school and a training college for teachers. The 1929 edition of *The Child in the Church* includes pictures of their materials about the liturgy, the symbols of the liturgical seasons, and the life of Christ.

Maria Montessori came to Ireland in 1927 to the Ursuline Convent, Waterford. The Convent of Mercy had St. Oteran's School which was a large National School. They had converted their school for young children to the Montessori Method, and in the 1929 edition of *The Child in the Church*, there are pictures of their sensorial materials for Montessori religious education as well.

The Dominican Convent, Sion Hill, Blackrock, Dublin, Ireland, is of special interest. In 1928 Montessori gave a course in Dublin to representatives of over a dozen Dominican Convents. Thirty years later, Sofia Cavalletti was invited to give lectures there.

Writing in the 1965 edition of *The Child in the Church*, Cavalletti graciously gave her hosts credit for their contributions to her work: "Some of this has been copied from the Dominican Sisters at the Sion Hill Convent, Blackrock, Dublin—and from other material devised by members of the Catholic Montessori Guild in England."[48]

Cavalletti then went on to suggest what her own contributions had been to that point. First, she added the parables. In her format, a child carries out the action with wooden figures while another reads the text. "Such figures were presented in a more or less abstract manner in order to differentiate them from the figures used in the Christmas or Easter panorama, since these latter stand for definite historical persons."

Secondly, she had added several kinds of three-dimensional models. One was a plaster model of Jerusalem for lessons about Holy Week. She also created a model of the Lake of Tiberias and one of the whole of Palestine. A picture in the same edition of the *Child in the Church* also shows her model of the tomb. She has continued to experiment, create many additional materials, and expand the theoretical base for this approach to the present day. (See below for more information on Cavalletti.)

THE LEGACY OF E. M. STANDING

On February 26, 1962, Sister Margaret Jane of Mount St. Vincent's in Seattle wrote to Standing at McCarthy's Hotel in Fethard, County Tipperary, Ireland. She invited and then "ordered" him to come to Seattle to live. She said, "I want it well understood that you are to be our guest here in this house as long as you wish—absolutely free of charge."[49]

He wrote in his journal on May 28, 1962, recalling Dante, that his "*Vita Nuova* begins." E. M. Standing was about seventy-five years old when he crossed the Atlantic on the Queen Elizabeth to begin his new life. On June 3 he wrote that he saw "snow clad mountains in the distance." The end of his journey by train to Seattle was near.

Standing's last years were very active. *The Montessori Method: A Revolution in Education*[50] came out in 1962. He had been working again on *The Child in the Church* since 1960, and the new version was published in 1965. In addition, Standing and Fr. William Codd, S.J., a professor of education and psychology at Seattle University, set up a Montessori training program at the University.

E. M. Standing died March 4, 1967. Letters of sadness came to Seattle University from all over the world. He left a good portion of his estate, including royalties from the sale of his books, to support the Seattle University Montessori Teacher Education Program. He also left a legacy of love and respect for children and their religious life, as well as his fair and passionate "impressions" of his Montessori vocation.

THE THIRD GENERATION: SOFIA CAVALLETTI

Sofia Cavalletti was born in Rome on August 21, 1917, in the very room where she now has her study. The apartments, descending from her mother's side of the family, have been near the Piazza Navona for many generations. This is also the building in which Eugenio Pacelli was born. He was elected Pope Pius XII on his birthday in March of 1939 at the briefest conclave in Church history: one day and three ballots.

Two people in particular have influenced Cavalletti's professional life: Maria Montessori and Eugenio Zolli. Zolli, born Israel Zoller, was at one time the Chief Rabbi of Rome, having come to Rome from Trieste in 1938 at the age of fifty-seven. On his mother's side of the family there had been rabbis and scholars for over two centuries.

When the Germans took over Rome in 1943, the persecution of the Jews became more severe and more systematic. Zolli and his wife, Emma Maionica, went into hiding. In his biography, *Before the Dawn*, he wrote that their daughter, Miriam, was "ferocious" as she moved her parents, paralyzed by the complexity of the situation, to seek shelter.

Part of the situation's complexity was that Zolli's religious life was deeply conflicted. The difficulty was finally resolved on February 13, 1945, when he and his wife were baptized as Roman Catholics in a small chapel inside Santa Maria degli Angeli, located near the Piazza della Republica. He took as his baptismal name Eugenio Maria, paying homage to the reigning pontiff, Pius XII.

Zolli lived the rest of his life at the Gregoriana in Rome, where he went to mass every morning and stayed afterwards to pray. He taught Semitic studies and Biblical exegesis in the Gregorian Pontifical University in Rome and at other places in the city.

Sofia Cavalletti first met Zolli in 1946 in a class at the University of Rome. She was struck by the connection he drew between the prophets and the beatitudes of Jesus. Although he taught that Christianity completed Judaism, it was his purity of heart that left a lasting impression on Cavalletti. This was the beginning of Cavalletti's deep love of the Hebrew Scriptures and her interest in Jewish-Christian relations. She would find that purity of heart again in her work with children.

Sofia Cavalletti became one of the first women to earn the *laurea* from the *Universita della Sapienza* in Rome in her speciality. The *laurea* is a four-year general degree with two more years of specialization. Her specialization was in "The Philology, Culture and History of Ancient Eastern Semitic Languages." When Zolli died on March 2, 1956, she was asked to write several of the tributes to him.

In the spring of 1954, two years after Montessori's death, a friend brought her seven-year-old son to Cavalletti for some lessons about religion.[51] They were joined then or soon after by two others. The joyful response of the children to her opening of the Bible and talking seriously with them about God began her journey to appreciate the child's relationship with God and the art of nourishing that powerful potential.

Cavalletti's interest and ability as a teacher of children did not go unnoticed by the energetic Signorina Costa Gnocchi, who had started a Montessori School at Palazzo Taverna in Rome. She persuaded Cavalletti to teach religion at her school.

Gianna Gobbi brought the knowledge of Montessori to mix with Cavalletti's knowledge about the Bible. Signorina Gobbi also was teaching in the school at Palazzo Taverna. She and Cavalletti soon attracted so many children to their religion classes that their work was moved to its present site in the Cavalletti apartments at 34 Via Degli Orsini in Rome. Together they worked with children and trained adults for this kind of spiritual formation until Gobbi's death in 2001.

The year 1956 shows a shift in Cavalletti's bibliography from writing mainly book reviews to publishing her own original work. This was the year that Eugenio Zolli died and Cavalletti's article "L'itinerario spirituale di Eugenio Zolli" ("The Spiritual Itinerary of Eugenio Zolli") appeared.[52] In 1957 Cavalletti was asked to give a paper at the International Montessori Congress in Rome. This meeting introduced her to Montessorians from around the world for the first time.

In 1958 the international scope of her work expanded with a trip to Dublin to give a course for teachers. Her visits to the United States, Canada, Mexico, Germany, Greece and elsewhere have continued to expand the awareness of what she and her colleagues have discovered at the Center in Rome.

Against the background of new openness in the Catholic Church—Pope John XXIII convoked the Second Vatican Council on December 25, 1961—Cavalletti published *Educazione religiosa, liturgia e metodo Montessori* (*Religious Education, Liturgy and the Montessori Method*). In this work, she traced the history of this approach and described the work of her Center to date. In addition to the experiments of Montessori in Barcelona, she mentioned the Benedictine Sisters of the Congregation of Mount Olivet (near Antwerp) as the "first to experiment with the proposed material for the teaching of the Mass."

Cavalleti also noted Catholic Montessori schools in Holland, particularly in Rotterdam. She described the Convent of the Assumption and the Regina Pacis School in London, and the work of the Dominican Sisters and the Sacred Heart Convent in Dublin. The Catholic Association for Montessori Education was mentioned, as were courses given in Calcutta and Colombo. She made special mention of Michel Lanternier's work in France, first at Limoges and then at Rennes, where the whole school's life was centered around the mass and the liturgical year.

In 1963 the international organization *L'Associazione "Maria Montessori" per la formazione religiosa del bambino* (The Maria Montessori Association for the Religious Formation of the Child) was founded. Today Cavalletti's Center in Rome remains at the heart of this network.

CAVALLETTI'S VISION

Cavalletti has called her approach a "method of signs." A sign, like a butterfly, is destroyed when it is pinned to a board and classified. The wings are still there but it cannot fly. The way to keep signs alive is to show children how to meditate on them.

This is not an invitation to enter into a private flight of fantasy. It is an invitation to enter more deeply into reality. Cavalletti wrote:

> In order to pierce the meaning of the parable we need to work with our imagination and our intuition. We need to use our imagination because we must not move away from the images through which the parable reveals reality to us. The author of the parable has not worked with fantasy; the likeness he is suggesting to us between the two levels of reality is not his own personal creation, nor is it a literary contrivance; it is an ontological likeness: The Kingdom of God can be compared to a mustard seed because the seed *is* in some way a bearer of the reality of the kingdom.[53]

Cavalletti is not proposing an approach that teaches the answers to life's theological questions. She is giving children the signs as instruments that are peripheral to the center but take one into the center of the relationship with God. "Slowly, as we go deeper into the heart of things by concentrating on one point, we will come to realize, with infinite wonder, that the global vision of reality becomes always greater."[54]

THE ACHIEVEMENT OF CAVALLETTI

The work of Sofia Cavalletti and her associates has made four primary contributions to the Montessori tradition of religious education:

- expansion of an integrated curriculum
- formation of an international organization
- provision of an ecumenical spirit
- development of an explicit theological base

First, Cavalletti's expansion of the Montessori religious education curriculum has been enormous. The Association's courses in the United States, for example, divide the work into three developmental stages. Each level might have as many as forty or fifty presentations alone. Most of the presentations use specific sensorial materials. This "spiral curriculum" has been integrated by the Montessori custom of defining the indirect preparation, direct preparation, the direct aims and indirect aims for each presentation. Cavalletti and her colleagues have added specific points of doctrine to this custom.

Second, the international organization is a loose confederation of people with a shared vision that respects the child and supports the child's religious formation. At the same time, it is a community of people who respect each other and seek to know the child in and among themselves as a way to come closer to God. The thirtieth anniversary gathering in Rome was not just Roman parents, former students and friends. There were also representatives from the many national associations around the world. Today there are children who have grown up in these classes and who now are becoming leaders and friends of this organization.

Third, Cavalletti also added an ecumenical spirit not present in the first two generations of the tradition. Before Cavalletti, the Montessori Movement was at the same time too inclusive and too exclusive to foster an ecumenical experiment. As the Montessori Movement became more and more international, the ties to the Roman Catholic Church became problematic. Questions and materials about specific religions were no longer included in the training of teachers because of the respect for the variety of religions and denominations involved.

Standing, on the other hand, wanted to stress the Roman Catholic connection. He placed a picture of Benedictus XV in the front of the 1929 edition of *The Child in the Church* and placed a quotation about Maria Montessori by Pope John XXIII in the 1965 edition. At the close of the 1965 edition he also included a plea for the restoration of the Catholic Montessori Guild in England to coordinate Catholic Montessori activities.

Standing wrote that the Guild had "been inactive for some years chiefly due to the circumstance that most of those who were active in propagating it have recently gone to live in the United States of America."[55] (Standing was referring primarily to himself and to Mother Isabel Eugenia.) Leadership in Cavalletti's Association is much less dependent on a few leaders living in a single country.

The spirit of Vatican II still pervades the Association in Rome both in its openness and in its theology, to which we will turn in a moment. Today in the United States, interest ranges across denominational lines, although this is not as true in other countries.

Fourth, Cavalletti has also provided a foundational theology for the method. In 1936 the seed of this theology was planted, when the world was changing. As Sofia Cavalletti was about to enter her twenties, the Austrian Jesuit Josef Andreas Jungmann published his *Die Frohbotschaf und unsere Glaubensverkundigung* (*The Good News and our Proclamation of Belief*).[56]

Jungmann was a great liturgical scholar who felt compelled to write about religious education. He urged that religious education move from the scholastic-laden catechism approach inherited from previous centuries to the announcement of the event of Christ's birth, death and resurrection (kerygma) and the implications of this for salvation history. The book was admired by European catechists, but many theologians were negative and argued for it to be condemned. At the direction of the Jesuit superior general, the book was merely withdrawn from the market, an action to which the Holy Office responded with gratitude.[57]

On the surface Jungmann was asking for a pastoral shift to a greater emphasis on scripture and liturgy, and away from scholastic definitions and the memorization of catechisms. The theological challenge went deeper. The theologians were not yet willing to come to grips with the question of the nature of revelation in the modern world.

Jungmann understood salvation history from the point of view of a liturgist rather than as a dogmatic theologian or biblical scholar. He focused more on the centrality of the mass, while Protestants focused more on the historical Christ. The salvation history view had completely carried the day in Catholic theology by 1963 when Jungmann published *Glaubensverkundigung im Lichte der Frohbotschaft* (*Proclamation in the Light of the Good News*)[58] which reiterated and redefined many of the arguments he had first put forward in 1936. By now this was the theme of Vatican II and Jungmann's work was fully accepted.

In 1961 Cavalletti noted Jungmann only twice in her book *Educazione religiosa, liturgia e metodo Montessori* (*Religious Education, Liturgy and Montessori Method*). She agreed that the intuition of God's love in Christ needed to come before entering into either the explicit study of the Ten Commandments or the Catechism. In the "Preface" Cyprian Vagaggini, O.S.B. noted the work of Jungmann and Hofinger among others and the twenty-five year emphasis on "the pedagogical force of the liturgy."

In December, 1962, Cavalletti wrote in *L'Osservatore Romano*[59] about the "liturgical nature" of the Montessori method and explained "why such a method is coming to be considered with a particular interest at a time in which a catechetical renewal finds its place in the vast picture of the liturgical renaissance." The influence of the liturgical and kerygmatic renewal is clear not only in the materials and presentations Cavalletti and Gobbi developed, but also in the books Cavalletti prepared for her training courses in Rome. They are being translated into English now.

CONCLUSION

Cavalletti, Standing and Montessori all seemed to sense the child's profound need to be in contact with the wonder and love of God. It is not out of compensation that the child turns to God and finds such joy. It is because God nourishes the child in a way that helps the child sense his or her true nature. The Montessori tradition of religious education has developed a powerful way to help do this. As Cavalletti says: "In helping the child's religious life, far from imposing something that is foreign to him, we are responding to the child's silent request: 'Help me to come closer to God by myself'."[60]

REFLECTING: ENTERING THE TRADITION

You can now see why I stress the continuity of Godly Play with this tradition. Let's reflect on the story of the Montessori tradition of religious education:

• I wonder what part of this story you like best?

....

....

....

• I wonder what part is the most important part?

....

....

....

• I wonder where you are in this story or what part of it is especially about you?

....

....

....

• I wonder if there is any of this experience we can leave out and still have all the tradition we need?

....

....

CHAPTER 7
TOWARD A THEOLOGY OF CHILDHOOD*

GOD WAS IN THIS PLACE

Our family moved from the East Coast to the West Coast when our daughters were six and eight years old. After a few months of being separated from dad, who was already working out west, we were able to join him just before the new school year started. Cardboard boxes were everywhere, and the girls enthusiastically wanted to unpack and set up their new rooms. After hours of cardboard and newsprint, I checked in on our hardworking girls.

Charlotte, the eldest, was busily taping pictures of her Massachusetts buddies onto the newly painted walls. What I found next to her bed was amazing. Over her bedside table she had draped an old piece of red velvet that we had used to line a drawer. On top of it were our creche figures of the Holy Family, cow and donkey, and a UNICEF collection box from the previous Halloween. "What's this?" I asked, truly wondering.

"I wanted to have my own special place to talk to God until I know my way around," she said simply. And God was in this place, too...

—Sally Thomas, Godly Play Trainer

The Godly Play classroom is planned and maintained for the sake of the children's community gathered there. We don't go there to get our own needs met, but to minister to the needs of the children entrusted to our care. However, most Godly Play teachers will tell you, with joy, how enriched they have been through this style of teaching. Many religious education directors struggle with high teacher turnover, even teacher burnout. In contrast, directors of Godly Play programs find that teachers themselves feel nurtured by the Godly Play methods and tend to want to deepen their commitment rather than end it.

In some sense, this chapter is meant to address the playful question, "What's in it for you?" As you enter into or deepen your Godly Play ministry, what benefits might you gain from your involvement? I suggest that one significant benefit of Godly Play teaching is that we become genuinely mature human beings through our ministry: that is, we enter the kingdom of heaven that Jesus promised us. How do we get to that, and what does that mean? These are questions best addressed through a theology of childhood for adults, which we turn to now.

*Funding for researching this chapter was generously provided by the Lily Endowment.

REFLECTING: CHILDHOOD MEMORIES

First, I'll invite you to reflect on childhood memories. Sit back. Relax. Put your feet on the floor and your hands at your sides. Loosely gather you hands in your lap. Close your eyes. Let your mind wander.

Now go back in time to when you could not see over the table:

• What was it like when you had to stand on tiptoe to reach a doorknob?

....

....

....

....

....

• What was your room like? Did you have to climb up to get into bed?

....

....

....

....

....

• Where was the center of warmth in your house?

....

....

....

....

....

• Listen for voices from childhood. Who is speaking?

....

....

....

....

- What do you see out your window? Do you stand on something to see out?

....
....
....

- Who really cared for you when you were a child?

....
....
....
....

- Were you ever in the hospital? What were the sounds? The smells?

....
....
....
....

- Did you ever have to move to a new house? How big were you then?

....
....
....

- Were you ever hurt? What happened?

....
....
....
....

- Were you ever lost? Where? Were you found? How? By whom?

....
....
....

i wonder

- What is something you never could really understand when you were little?

....

....

....

....

- What did your church smell like?

....

....

....

....

- Did you go to Sunday school? Who took you?

....

....

....

....

- Did you have a hard time finding your way to the rooms?

....

....

....

- How did you get up and down the stairs? Did you have to take big steps?

....

....

....

- What were the colors in the room?

....

....

....

- Do you remember any of the teachers?

....

....

....

....

- What did the tables, chairs or other furniture feel like? What was on the walls?

....

....

....

....

- What happened there? Can you hear the voices?

....

....

....

....

....

Reflect on these experiences in a way that is appropriate for you. How have they influenced your life? What do they have to do with your involvement with children today?

CHRISTIAN AMBIGUITY TOWARD CHILDREN

There is ambivalence in the thought and practice of the Christian Church about children. I'll characterize the opposing feelings the Church holds about children as a "high view" and a "low view." We idealize children and yet we demonize them. We celebrate a "year of the child" and exclude children from worship. We value them, yet spend relatively little time or money on their needs. We tout evangelism to add members, but we do not count children, already present in the Church, to be worth "evangelizing" or even the hospitality we give to strangers.

These notes about a theology of childhood are an invitation to both pray and discuss a theology that is based on an explicitly high view of children. Both prayer and critical thinking are needed to deal with this ambivalence. We need prayer to be open to our ambivalence and to the damage it does to children and congregations. We also need our critical reasoning to clarify what has contaminated our verbal and nonverbal communication about and with children.

We begin our critical thinking by trying to understand why the Church has never, or very seldom, held a high view of children. Today may be one of the few times in the history of theology since Jesus that children can be seen for who they are.

The second step faces the problem, which almost halts the project before it can begin. Jesus was clear that adults had to become like children to enter the Kingdom, but he did not define the child whom we are to be like. This means that we need to consult two kinds of texts to write a theology of childhood. One text is words. The other text is children.

Thirdly, we will interpret with a high view what the gospels tell us about Jesus and children. This will generate eight issues that a theology of childhood needs to take into consideration.

These eight issues will be developed and synthesized into three propositions:
• the theological journey as Hide-and-Seek
• the importance of nonverbal communication
• the human need for an ethic of blessing

WHY HAS THERE BEEN NO THEOLOGY OF CHILDHOOD?

There are eight primary reasons why there has been no major theology of childhood in the history of the Church. While no single reason has prevented attention from being given to this subject, the combination of these eight reasons has blinded us to this absence.

SCRIPTURAL SCARCITY

First of all, there is little basis in scripture for such a theology. Only about eight bits of evidence from Jesus' sayings and reported action in the synoptic gospels exist to anchor such speculation.

Scriptural scarcity, however, has not limited theological speculation in other areas. For example, there is little direct basis in scripture for such elevated doctrines as the *Imago Dei* or the Holy Trinity. The *Imago Dei* is based primarily on Genesis 1:26: "Then God said, "Let us make man in our image, after our likeness.""

In the case of the Holy Trinity there is no specific reference in scripture, although the raw narrative material is there to base it on. The concept of the Holy Trinity developed because of inconsistent narratives, which referred to God as Jesus, the Holy Spirit and Creator. Under the pressure of Greek philosophy in the fourth century, these three ways of speaking of God were coordinated despite their differences by the new logic of the Holy Trinity.

The *Imago Dei* and Holy Trinity have become useful as well as venerable doctrines despite little scriptural basis. A theology of childhood, therefore, should not be disqualified for this reason.

LOW VIEW OF WOMEN

The second reason there has not been a theology of childhood is that for many centuries the political church has held a low opinion of women. Ironically this view has sometimes been combined with a very idealistic view of Mary, angels and saintly (that is, nonsexual and totally giving) women. Children, who have so recently come through "those lowly gates," as Tertullian put it, are closely associated with women, so they too have been held in low esteem "by association." Like women, children have also, at times, been impossibly idealized by Christian art and culture despite the dark view of children the theologians have taken. The image of the Christ Child is, perhaps, at the root of this, although in some art the infant looks like an ageless adult to represent the Logos.

One of the most promising areas of health in today's political church has been the reexamination of the inherited assumptions about women. The Church in our time may be more ready than ever before to see women and the children so closely associated with them more clearly. This shift of perspective has helped clear the way for a theology of childhood.

LOW VIEW OF CHILDREN

A third reason that there has not yet been a theology of childhood is that children have been dismissed as "mere children." Children are characterized as powerless and lacking in adult knowledge and experience. But children are only "low" when the standard for comparison is adult strength. Jesus turns this standard of comparison on its head.

Children today are often acknowledged only as "the Church of the future," a kind of formless clay to be shaped by the Church's teaching. It follows from this assumption that there is little we adults can learn from them, despite Jesus' view. The test case for this is the *de facto* exclusion of children from Holy Communion in many churches, despite their baptism and despite a formal welcoming of them into the community. This attitude is at odds with observing them carefully as they receive Holy Communion in order to learn from them how to truly receive the sacrament.

The low view of children is intensified by the doctrine of original sin, which was emphasized by Saint Augustine. He saw children as creatures with reason so corrupted that they cannot know the truth, and a will so diseased that even if they could know the truth they would not be able to do it. The view of child-rearing which follows from this is that adults must break children's blind and sometimes belligerent will to prepare the way for the manifestation of God's grace.

The low view of children held by most theologians since Augustine is hard to square with Jesus' high view of children. Why would Jesus counsel us to become like children if only the low view were true? Actually, both the low and the high views have merit. Karl Rahner is one of the few theologians, if not the only one, who has been able to keep the tension between the high and low views of children alive. More will be said about this tension below.

POWER STRUCTURES

A fourth reason for the lack of interest in a theology of childhood has to do with the invisible structures in society which keep the powerless marginal and the oppressed in their place. These structures of power are supported even by people of good will, and even when they are working to help the marginalized and the oppressed.

In our culture, many Christians and non-Christians alike are eager to say what is politically correct about children, but they do not take the steps to truly change the fundamental structures that continue to marginalize children. The *status quo* is so deeply assumed that alternative suggestions seem mindless and silly!

For example, our nation continues to spend vastly more money on the military and on prisons than we spend on helping families and schools rear our children to be competent, intelligent, strong, creative and wise peacemakers. The gap between what we spend on war "to keep peace" and warehousing criminals and what we spend on education, children's health and family viability is difficult to reconcile, but it is literally *unthinkable* to argue seriously that our present approach to "domestic tranquility" is either cost effective or ethical.

CHURCH POLITICS

A fifth reason why we have not had a theology of childhood in the Church is because of what our political church asks of our theologians. They are trained and called on to speak for and to the political church about the Church's identity. They inevitably become involved in the power structures of society of which the political church is a part.

In addition, theologians often engage politically with adults within their own teaching faculties. How could they not? They are leaders. This involvement also tends to focus their awareness on controlling institutional power, much as Jesus' disciples assumed that his Kingdom was political. The "naïve," open, personal power that Jesus showed and demonstrated in his relations with children, as well as with others, is often discounted as a serious political option.

A classical case, showing the involvement of theologians in the power structures of society and the political church, is the part theologians played in the four General Councils during the fourth and fifth centuries. The process by which the fundamental statement of Christian theology was worked out was deeply involved with imperial rulers and the overt or implied use of force. At the same time it is very important to note that the doctrines worked out during those centuries are masterpieces, which continue to renew the Church. God remains God.

Theologians also support and help refine our pastoral care. But this too has been clearly dominated by adult concerns. A recent exception to adult dominance in pastoral care is the early work of Andrew Lester, which took the lead in advocating for and informing the pastoral care of children. The continuing lack of publications about the pastoral care of children, when compared to those about adults, argues that there is still comparatively little interest among clergy for such books.

In addition to their involvement with the power of church and culture, theologians are also persons of prodigious memory as well as powerful and quick intellect. They spend years developing these abilities as well as acquiring fluency in modern and ancient languages, the history of theology and the logic of ancient rhetoric and modern argument. Our theologians are great souls, who combine brilliant talents with an enormous capacity for service. They are impressive human beings, but one cannot do everything. Their talent and character moves them in a particular direction, a direction not especially useful for getting to know the silent child, the other "text" that Jesus put in the midst of the disciples to teach them and us about the Kingdom.

DIFFICULT QUESTIONS

A sixth reason there has not been a theology of childhood is because of the real difficulty of the questions children raise. It is not easy to discover and speak about their spirituality. One needs to be patient and wait for them to reveal themselves at their own time and in their own way. We are often in too great a hurry to know them well, so we use methods to *investigate* their lives, even though the very process of investigation can distort our knowledge of who they truly are.

Our great hurry and need to quantify our research moves us toward a lack of appreciation for the "quality of being" in the relationships children have with God, their deep self, with others (including ourselves) and with nature. We want to count, weigh and measure. It is easier to quantify the bags of rice or wheat and the containers of milk loaded on a ship or sent down the street than it is to understand the spirituality of the those who will eat and drink what we send them.

If it is true that human spirituality is located in nonverbal communication, then it is the special province of theologians to articulate this. A theology of childhood is important because it is an effort to hear what children communicate, even when they have no words to say what they mean.

CULTURAL CONSTRUCTS

A seventh reason we have not yet had a theology of childhood is because the *concept* of childhood appears to be, at least in part, a cultural construct. It changes and is relative to time and place.

Of course, all children begin to speak about the age of two years and they can create and bear children from about twelve years of age. This is true regardless of the culture into which the child is born or within which it is reared. Still, what the period between those two biological markers means is what we need to know if we are to be like children.

The history of childhood, then, is required reading for those who struggle to "become like a child." We need the perspective of history to see the assumptions of our own time more clearly by contrasting them with ages past.

SINGLE DEVELOPMENTAL PERIOD

Finally, there has been no theology of childhood, because it seems absurd to build a theology on what is unique to a single developmental period. This only seems absurd, however, until one realizes that we already do that. Our present theology is by and for adults; it bears the assumptions of and communication forms of adults.

For most people only a few of these eight reasons are enough to cause them to give up trying to be like a child. It is too complicated. We grow impatient and use adult concerns to guide our journey. Yet, according to Jesus, this approach is an error. We must, therefore, take the time, despite our resistance, to consider more closely what Jesus' remarkable view of children is, so we can consider the theological propositions it generates.

DEFINING THE "CHILD" WE ARE TO BE LIKE

The definition of the child depends on which language domain one is using. Historians have found that the meaning of childhood has changed over the centuries.

Psychologists have found that children change over a lifetime. Educators have been the most optimistic about children's natural abilities, especially since the eighteenth century.

Jean-Jacques Rousseau (1712–1778) greatly influenced the eighteenth century's high view of children. His *Emile or On Education*, published in 1762, was about the education of a naturally whole person who is to live in society, which tends to corrupt him. Rousseau's *The Confessions*, finished in 1770, is interesting to read alongside Augustine's *Confessions*, which was composed sometime around the last three years of the fourth century. While Augustine thought children began evil but could become good through baptism and grace, Rousseau thought children were born good and became evil by involvement in society.

In the Latin of Augustine's day, his book *Confessions* was titled by a word which meant both praise and penitence. In Rousseau's *The Confessions* there is little penitence. Henry Chadwick noted in an understated way that, "The men of the Enlightenment thought the actual perfecting of man was hindered by belief in original sin and disliked Augustine very much."[61] From the eighteenth century on, children began to be thought about more in secular terms and as a group with special needs different from adults, such as healthcare and civilizing.

It takes us too far afield to present the views of children by the historians, the psychologists and the educators, but we must say something about the view of theologians because it has had so much influence on the Church and Western civilization. We will begin with Saint Paul.

Paul used the child as an image of what is "less than adult." This is fair enough, because such a view is factually true. Children do lack the experience, the vocabulary and the cognitive abilities of adults, but Paul's use of the image of the child in this way obscured the truth of Jesus' high view. Paul used the analogy of children like this:

- He contrasted the spiritual to the fleshly, using the child as an example of the fleshly, which is negative (1 Corinthians 3:1).
- In the same letter (1 Corinthians 13:11) children and adults were contrasted in terms of knowledge. Paul used the child as the example of less knowledge.
- Paul also compared the Thessalonians to children who are helpless (1 Thessalonians 2:7). He and his colleagues are like nurses to them.
- In the Letter to the Galatians (4:3) Paul compared the pre-Christian period to the present time. The present time is like the time when the heir takes full power and possession over his inheritance by adoption. Before this legal vesting, however, one is like a child, a slave to the elemental spirits of the universe.

I'm not claiming that Paul disliked or was unaware of children's gifts; I am only saying that he did not use the image of a child as Jesus did, as the image of one who can teach adults how to become mature.

Saint Paul's reduction of Jesus' view into the commonly held view of his time and place dropped the tension between the truth of the child's lack of experience and less-than-adult reasoning and the truth of Jesus' view of the child's ability to teach adults about their own maturity. Not until the twentieth century and the theology of Karl Rahner was this tension restored. First, though, we must elaborate a bit more about the view of children Saint Augustine bequeathed to theology.

Aurelius Augustinus (354–430) lived all but five years of his life in Roman North Africa. He was bishop of the busy seaport Hippo for the last thirty-four years of his life. Chadwick tells us that throughout his life Augustine was interested in the study of infant behavior to better understand human nature. An example of Augustine's interest in children may be taken from his *Confessions*. No creature is more selfish than a baby is, he wrote. "If infants do no injury, it is for lack of strength, not for lack of will."

Augustine's method for the study of human nature was very unlike ours today. In the *Confessions* he wrote, as Chadwick translates it:

> I have personally watched and studied a jealous baby. He could not yet speak and, pale with jealousy and bitterness, glared at his brother sharing his mother's milk. Who is unaware of this fact of experience? Mothers and nurses claim to charm it away by their own private remedies. But it can hardly be innocence, when the source of milk is flowing richly and abundantly, not to endure a share going to one's blood brother, who is in profound need, dependent for life exclusively on that one food.[62]

Augustine is more concerned to make an elegant rhetorical point than a statement of objective study, as we would think of it today. Despite Augustine's recognized ability to fathom human emotions, here he may be engaged in projection. He saw what he could not remember but suspected about *himself*, that the deep defect of human nature was there from the start. One wonders what the theological history of infant damnation might have been like if Augustine had picked up the baby and held it? What if he patted it on the back and the baby burped? Perhaps, the evil was only gas? The baby's "evil" could be a natural developmental category rather than a theological category.

Most theologians, writing about children since Paul and Augustine, have taken a low view of children, but a positive view begins to emerge in the nineteenth century. Friedrich Schleiermacher (1768–1834) in Germany and Horace Bushnell (1802–1876) in the United States took the minority view.

Schleiermacher addressed the theme of childhood in his *Soliloquies* (1800), his novella *Celebration of Christmas* (1806) and his *Sermons on the Christian Household* (1820). Meanwhile, on this continent, Bushnell's *Christian Nurture* (1861) was heavily criticized. Margaret Bendroth has noted his emphasis on "companionship, play and emotional intimacy between parents and children."[63] Both Schleiermacher and Bushnell seemed to have genuinely enjoyed family life and the company of children.

In our own times, Karl Rahner (1904–1984), a German Jesuit, has produced the most eloquent and best-balanced view of children among theologians. He wrote even less than Schleiermacher and Bushnell did, but in a single essay, "Ideas for a Theology of Childhood," he developed a remarkable and carefully nuanced synthesis of the doctrine of original sin with Jesus' high view of children.[64]

Mary Ann Hinsdale, a noted scholar, tells us that Rahner's ideas about children were first presented as a lecture given on October 1, 1962, at the Second International Conference of "SOS Children's Villages" in Hinterbuhl, near Vienna, shortly before the opening of the Second Vatican Council. It was later published in the pastoral journal *Geist und Leben*.[65]

To provide some background to what Rahner has to say, let us first note that in the scriptures there are 285 references to "child," five references to "childhood," 740 references to "children," and fifteen references to "children of God," which refers primarily to adults.[66] Most of these references are used in direct address such as "my child" to instruct someone of lesser knowledge or merely to identify a young person as in "if your child asks for a fish" (Luke 11:11). There is no definition of a child or of childhood among these references.

Rahner's approach to the definition problem, which he identified, was to supplement scriptural studies by looking at the children around him and remembering his own childhood. He also included the study of references to "children of God" and worked backward from these remarks about adults to the kind of child they appeared to be like!

Rahner's conclusion was that a child of God is an adult who approaches life with radical openness. He wrote that in children the "transcendence of faith, hope and love in which the ultimate essence of the basic act of religion precisely consists is already *ipso facto* an achieved and present fact." This is a way of living, as he goes on to say, that "the skeptics and those who have made shipwreck of their lives bitterly describe as 'naïve'." The real test of adult maturity for Rahner is to enter the "wonderful adventure of remaining a child forever" and seeking to become "a child to an ever increasing extent."

In spite of leaving us only a single, brief treatise on the subject, we must not overlook the importance Rahner gave to the theology of childhood. He wrote that this project was not to engage in "petty sentimentality," and it goes "beyond pedagogy," the field of Christian education to which the subject is usually dismissed by theologians. The value of a theology of childhood for Rahner was nothing less than the project of "perfecting and saving humanity."

To restore the balance between the low and high views of children in theology we turn now to Jesus and the children. We will approach this interpretative task as if the heavy weight of theology were not present. Let's begin anew with Jesus and his high view of children.

JESUS' REMARKABLE VIEW OF CHILDREN

The evidence about Jesus' view of children is slim but potent. Only eight primary references to Jesus and children are to be found in the gospels. Still, this provides more than enough material with which to write a book; Hans-Reudi Weber's *Jesus and the Children* is one excellent example.[67] A shorter but still splendid treatment of this material is Judith Gundry-Volf's "The Least and the Greatest: Children in the New Testament," a chapter in Bunge's *The Child in Christian Thought*.[68]

If one takes a low view of children, there is a tendency to interpret the texts about Jesus and the children as meaning that *even* children are included in the Kingdom, despite their lowly status. If one takes a high view of children, the inclination is to notice what the children disclose by being children, who are already included in the Kingdom. They thus show what adults need in order to be mature (enter the Kingdom).

I will take a high view, but the low view also is true. The danger of the low view is to miss Jesus' unique view of children. The danger for the high view is to romanticize them. We need both views, but the high view has been largely overlooked so I will emphasize it in this chapter. I propose to restore the tension between the two views, which most theologians since Paul have allowed to wither away.

Our discussion will be structured for the most part as a conversation with Weber. He identified and named four major themes for study. They are: "We Piped, And You Did Not Dance" (Matthew 11:16-19 and Luke 7:31-35), "Let the Children Come To Me" (Mark 10:13-16), "Unless You Become Like a Child" (Matthew 18:3, Mark 10:15 and Luke 18:17) and "A Child in the Midst of Them" (Matthew 18:1-5, Mark 9:33-37 and Luke 9:46-48). As you can see, Weber treated "Unless You Become Like a Child" as an independent saying and disconnected it from its narrative contexts for his study.

The principle Weber used to select the passages for his study was to include only those occasions where Jesus met actual children. What he calls "We Piped, And You Did Not Dance," however, does not fit his criterion, while the raising of Jairus' daughter does, yet he rejected it. His reasoning for excluding Jairus' daughter is that it is like other "miracles and healings,"[69] which make the age of the one raised irrelevant. Nonetheless I want to emphasize that Jesus *did* raise a young girl and did not limit his healing to adults.

THE PARABLE OF CHILDREN'S PLAY

Naming a passage already implies an interpretation, so it is interesting that the *Interpreter's Bible* calls this "The Parable of the Peevish Children." Weber calls it "The Parable of the Children's Game,"[70] a "polemic parable"[71] and "the game that failed."[72]

From Luke 7:31-35:

> To what then will I compare the people of this generation, and what are they like? They are like children sitting in the marketplace and calling to one another. "We played the flute for you, and you did not dance;
> > we wailed, and you did not weep."

> For John the Baptist has come eating no bread and drinking no wine, and you say, "He has a demon;" the Son of Man has come eating and drinking and you say, "Look, a glutton and a drunkard, a friend of tax collectors and sinners!" Nevertheless, wisdom is vindicated by all her children.

From Matthew 11:16-19:

> It is like children sitting in the marketplaces and calling to one another,
> > "We played the flute for you, and you did not dance;
> > > we wailed, and you did not mourn."

> For John came neither eating nor drinking, and they say, "He has a demon"; the Son of Man came eating and drinking, and they say, "Look, a glutton and a drunkard, a friend of tax collectors and sinners!" Yet wisdom is vindicated by her deeds.

Weber comments that when Jesus was a child he no doubt played in the marketplace himself. As an adult, he was also likely to have watched children playing there. Weber concludes that the parable shows Jesus' realistic view of children. He wrote: "Yet sometimes children sulk, and refuse to respond or understand."[73] He has not gone so far as to call the children "peevish" (complaining, irritable), but he does think this parable is about how they "refused to respond or understand." My question is about why they refused.

When you take a low view of children this saying merely puts down the adult listeners of Jesus. It does this by comparing them to children, who are assumed to be unable (perhaps because of defective reason) or unwilling (perhaps because of a diseased will) to listen to what they are told, learn from it and do what the adults have told them to do.

If we take the action out of the interpretative context about the bad adults and look at it as a freestanding event, the action of the children is more open to a high view.

Doing this allows us to take the parable as something adults can learn from rather than merely putting them down by a negative reference to children. What do the children know that we adults have forgotten? What are the clues in their behavior that can help us enter the Kingdom?

This is not to say that Jesus wouldn't get as angry or indignant about children's deafness as he does about the adult disciples' inability to hear what he says to them. He is fully capable of that. It is more about how he is with children in the rest of the eight core passages. All eight passages together make more sense when our assumption is that Jesus holds a high view of children.

Let's begin again, then. Let's assume a high view of children. What we have is the fact that the game did not take place. Why?

What is there about the children's play that can stop the game? In this case there is no evidence of an outside source for the problem. Nothing is said about the children misunderstanding the games proposed. No controversy about leadership among the children is mentioned. Neither was anything said about the games' rules or the children's understanding of them. If there is nothing extraneous to stop the game, then, what is there about play itself that may have stopped the game?

Let's return to Catherine Garvey's description of play: play is pleasurable, voluntary, done for itself, absorbing, and has connections with creativity, learning languages, learning social roles and problem-solving. Play, however, is difficult to *define* and remains somewhat ambiguous. For example, any activity done as play can also be done as nonplay. One can play with words, but words falter when it comes to signaling play. This is why so many researchers are content to work with only a description like Garvey's.

Play, however, can be divided into two kinds: "what-if play" and "as-if play."[74] As-if play is about adult roles, such as playing funeral or wedding feast. What-if play is about doing or thinking what has not been done or thought before. Isn't what-if play the kind of play it will take to know what the Kingdom is about, since it is completely new?

The children in the parable are presented with two kinds of as-if play, wedding feast and funeral. Their intuitive indifference toward such play is correct if this is a parable about the kind of play appropriate for knowing the Kingdom. In other words, if you want to play the game Jesus and John are playing; you need to use what-if play to discover it. This is because the Kingdom game is absolutely new, always new. It is about new life, so as-if play can't disclose it, even if you pretend to be like Jesus or John! It is a matter of creativity not mimicry.

If children have an ability to recognize the presence of the mystery of God as Creator, then, the children will know by intuition that the as-if play of preparing for adult roles (such as participating in weddings and funerals) is inappropriate. You cannot borrow conclusions about the Kingdom from someone else—even adults—and enter it. You need to make the journey yourself.

A CHILD IN THE MIDST OF THEM

The second text I would like to comment on is "A Child in the Midst of Them." Actually it is only in Matthew and Mark that Jesus sets the child in the midst of the disciples. In Luke he puts the child by his side. Nevertheless, in all three cases the child *remains silent*.

From Matthew 18:1-5:

> At that time the disciples came to Jesus and asked, "Who is the greatest in the kingdom of heaven?" He called a child, whom he put among them, and said, "Truly I tell you, unless, you change and become like children, you will never enter the kingdom of heaven. Whoever becomes humble like this child is the greatest in the kingdom of heaven. Whoever welcomes one such child in my name welcomes me."

From Mark 9:33-37:

> Then they came to Capernaum; and when he was in the house he asked them, "What were you arguing about on the way?" But they were silent, for on the way they had argued with one another who was the greatest. He sat down, called the twelve, and said to them, "Whoever wants to be first must be last of all and servant of all." Then he took a little child and put it among them; and taking it in his arms, he said to them, "Whoever welcomes one such child in my name welcomes me; and whoever welcomes me, welcomes not me but the one who sent me."

From Luke 9:46-48:

> And an argument arose among them as to which of them was the greatest. But Jesus, aware of their inner thoughts, took a child and put it by his side, and said to them, "Whoever welcomes this child in my name welcomes me, and whoever welcomes me welcomes the one who sent me; for the least among all of you is the greatest."

The silently eloquent "discourse on true greatness" by the child is reflected on by Jesus in two ways. First, he noted that the child lacks what is usually thought of as power and yet is able to enter (or receive) the Kingdom. Second, when you meet such a child you meet Jesus, the embodiment of the Kingdom. Many interpreters, such as the *Interpreter's Bible*, have focused on Jesus' "discourse." I prefer to focus on the child's silent teaching.

Of course children have a voice and can be noisy. The question this passage raises, however, is how deep our ontological appreciation is, despite such distractions. What do children teach us about maturity by their fundamental being?

LET THE CHILDREN COME

The third text we shall look at is "Let the Children Come." Why was Jesus "indignant?" The disciples were only trying to protect him, so he could do something more "important" than be with children. Children are weak and helpless. They do not have the life experience or cognitive ability to understand Jesus' teaching. Why should *they* deserve any special attention? Something like this must have been what the disciples thought, as many of Jesus' followers still think today!

From Matthew 19:13-15:

> Then little children were being brought to him in order that he might lay his hands on them and pray. The disciples spoke sternly to those who brought them; but Jesus said, "Let the little children come to me, and do not stop them; for it is to such as these that the kingdom of heaven belongs." And he laid his hands on them and went on his way.

From Mark 10:13-16:

> People were bringing little children to him in order that he might touch them; and the disciples spoke sternly to them. But when Jesus saw this, he was indignant and said to them, "Let the little children come to me; do not stop them; for it is to such as these that the kingdom of God belongs. Truly I tell you, whoever does not receive the kingdom of God as a little child will never enter it." And he took them up in his arms, laid his hands on them, and blessed them.

From Luke 18:15-17:

> People were bringing even infants to him that he might touch them; and when the disciples saw it, they sternly ordered them not to do it. But Jesus called for them and said, "Let the little children come to me, and do not stop them; for it is to such as these that the kingdom of God belongs. Truly I tell you, whoever does not receive the kingdom of God as a little child will never enter it."

When we turn our attention away from the adults in the parable and focus instead on the children Jesus received, we notice something ironic. They do not even care about adult experience or stages of cognitive ability. They know what they know about Jesus nonverbally. From their point of view, their knowledge of Jesus is not naïve. Perhaps this is one reason why children are in the Kingdom and many adults are not. Adults sometimes become so dependent on language to understand it they lose the power of the nonverbal knowing they were born with to enter the Kingdom.

Weber, however, carefully argues against this idea. For him the parable is not about the nature of children. Jesus included the little ones in the Kingdom not because of something positive about their nature.[75] It was *despite* their unworthiness. This is a parable, he argues, which is about the nature of God rather than the nature of children.

If we take a high view of children we notice something else. The ontological appreciation of the silent child, set in the midst of the talking adults, shows that the child bears revelation silently. In the New Testament, it is Paul, not children, who is the major model for an unworthy person being accepted by grace.

THE MILLSTONE TEXTS

The fourth text we shall consider was not commented on by Weber. I want to include it, because it clearly and passionately declares that hindering children from being children is a matter of life and death. This is because children are bearers of revelation for each other as well as for the adults around them.

This group of texts might be called "the millstone texts." They are found in Matthew 18:6-9, Mark 9:42-48 and Luke 17:1-2. All three prescribe an awful death to those who cause the little ones to stumble. Two of the three call for self-mutilation as well.

From Matthew 18:6-9:

> If any of you put a stumbling block before one of these little ones who believe in me, it would be better for you if a great millstone were fastened around your neck and you were drowned in the depth of the sea. Woe to the world because of stumbling blocks! Occasions for stumbling are bound to come, but woe to the one by whom the stumbling block comes! If your hand or your foot causes you to stumble, cut it off and throw it away; it is better for you to enter life maimed or lame than to have two hands or two feet and to be thrown into the eternal fire. And if your eye causes you to stumble, tear it out and throw it away; it is better for you to enter life with one eye than to have two eyes and to be thrown into the hell of fire.

From Mark 9:42-48:

> If any of you put a stumbling block before one of these little ones who believe in me, it would be better for you if a great millstone were hung around your neck and you were thrown into the sea. If your hand causes you to stumble, cut it off; it is better for you to enter life maimed than to have two hands and to go to hell, to the unquenchable fire. And if your foot causes you to stumble, cut it off; it is better to enter life lame than to have two feet and to be thrown into hell. And if your eye causes you to stumble, tear it out; it is better for you to enter the

kingdom of God with one eye than to have two eyes and to be thrown into hell, where their worm never dies, and the fire is never quenched.

From Luke 17:1-2:

Jesus said to his disciples, "Occasions for stumbling are bound to come, but woe to anyone by whom they come! It would be better for you if a millstone were hung around your neck and you were thrown into the sea than for you to cause one of these little ones to stumble."

These three texts can be connected with Jesus' indignation at the disciples who hindered the children from coming to him. Matthew connects this saying explicitly with "Let the Children Come To Me" while Mark and Luke locate the saying in different contexts but with the connection remaining at the implicit level. The different contexts do not change the meaning or the urgency of this saying. It is violent language about a matter of life and death.

BECOME LIKE A CHILD

The fifth text we will consider also "floats" in different contexts. Weber called this text "Become Like a Child" and isolated it as a freestanding saying. The text is about how children receive the Kingdom just as, Weber observed, they "beg" and "claim" food. The text occurs in two different contexts. In Matthew 18:3, the context is the discourse on true greatness. In Mark 10:15 and Luke 18:17, the context is Jesus' instruction to let the children come to him.

From Matthew 18:3:

Truly I tell you, unless you change and become like children, you will never enter the kingdom of heaven.

From Mark 10:15:

Truly I tell you, whoever does not receive the kingdom of God as a little child will never enter.

From Luke 18:17:

Truly I tell you, whoever does not receive the kingdom of God as a little child will never enter it.

This saying is not about children being more humble than adults are. It is about how adults do not realize that they remain in the same position as children in relation to life and death, even when they are adults. Weber calls this realization "objective humility."

Weber's book includes a brief survey as well as salient historical texts to show how people in the eastern half of the Mediterranean basin viewed education about the time of Jesus. Against this background he concluded that "A Child in the Midst of Them" is about the child teaching the disciples. Jesus' view was at odds with how adults in Rome, Greece and Jerusalem saw children and education. Weber believes this is a parable of reversal. I agree.

Weber connects Jesus' view of children with one of Jesus' general themes, the one about the first being last and the last being first. Seven times in the gospels, by his count, there are versions of this saying. His point is that the rhetoric of reversal is not only a characteristic of Jesus' communication but it is also a natural fact in the case of children. They teach "objective humility" to adults, if the adults can see beyond their customary interpretation of children as raw material for adult education.

Seeing beyond the low view of children, which prevails today as it did in antiquity, is, of course, the problem. The further irony in this situation is that adults need the intuitive ability of a child to recognize what the child has to teach. They need to meet children on their own ground and in their own way of knowing to understand what it is they need to enter the Kingdom.

We turn now to three texts where there is less attestation and less direct connection between Jesus and children. The texts are still related to Jesus and children, however, and to a theology of childhood.

BORN ANEW

In the sixth text (John 3:3, 5) we meet Nicodemus, who came by night and acknowledged Jesus as Rabbi. This suggests that for adults to enter the Kingdom they need to be born anew or be born "from above." Through Nicodemus, John has introduced the idea of a second naivete. This gives us a clue to just how much change is needed for adults to enter, receive or be in the Kingdom like a child. A total transformation is required. This is an all-encompassing existential discovery, not merely a matter of reason and will.

From John 3:3:

> Jesus answered him, "Very truly, I tell you, no one can see the kingdom of God without being born from above." Nicodemus said to him, "How can anyone be born after having grown old? Can one enter a second time into the mother's womb and be born?"

From John 3:5-8:

> Jesus answered, "Very truly, I tell you, no one can enter the kingdom of God without being born of water and Spirit. What is born of the flesh is flesh, and

what is born of the Spirit is spirit. Do not be astonished that I said to you, "You must be born from above." The wind blows where it chooses, and you hear the sound of it, but you do not know where it comes from or where it goes. So it is with everyone who is born of the Spirit.

The idea of the second naivete is one that will not be developed here, but it is rooted in the work of Jim Fowler in a psychological-theological way.[76]

THE CHILDREN CRY OUT

The seventh text we will comment on is one of the last two to be mentioned. Both of these texts are related to the power of children's intuition. In Matthew 21:15-16 we find Jesus cleansing the temple, healing there, and the children crying out, "Hosanna to the Son of David." The chief priests and scribes become angry and say to Jesus, "Do you hear what these are saying?"

From Matthew 21:15-16:

> But when the chief priests and the scribes saw the amazing things that he did, and heard the children crying out in the temple, "Hosanna to the Son of David," they became angry and said to him, "Do you hear what these are saying?" Jesus said to them, "Yes; have you never read,
> 'Out of the mouths of infants and nursing babies
> you have prepared praise for yourself'?"

The children knew something the chief priests and scribes did not want to admit or could not fathom. Jesus acknowledges this and quotes what was probably Psalm 8:2: "Thou whose glory above the heavens is chanted by the mouth of babes and infants..." They knew this by their nonverbal communication system, by which they intuited the discovery that they shouted as praise, using the most appropriate words they knew.

The context for this passage is about the cleansing of the temple. The children enter in Matthew (21:15-16), but the context is found in all four gospels: Matthew 21:12-17, Mark 11:15-19, Luke 19:45-46 and John 2:13-25.

REVEALED TO CHILDREN

The eighth text is also about children's intuition. The experience of the presence of God and the power it engenders in human beings can easily become a matter of pride. This distorts God's power by making it seem to be our own. Such a distortion is more likely to be made among "the wise and the intelligent" than it is among children who take God's presence for granted.

From Matthew 11:25-26:

> At that time Jesus said, "I thank you, Father, Lord of heaven and earth, because you have hidden these things from the wise and the intelligent and have revealed them to infants; yes, Father, for such was your gracious will."

From Luke 10:21:

> I thank you, Father, Lord of heaven and earth, because you have hidden these things from the wise and the intelligent and revealed them to infants; yes, Father, for that was your gracious will.

In Matthew this saying comes after the disciples of John have left to report what they have seen. Jesus then pronounces the woes on the cities and reflects on his knowledge of the Father. He invites all who labor and are heavy leaden to come to him, for he will give them rest. Here is the point: Jesus is as approachable as a child. Coming into his presence is very unlike coming into the presence of Augustus Caesar, Herod or a priest of the temple in Jerusalem. As with a child, distance and yet easy familiarity combine in Jesus' presence.

In Luke this saying is inserted in the narrative about the return of the seventy who have been amazed at their power. Jesus rejoiced at their childlike discovery, but he also warned them not to focus on this power as if it were their own. Instead, it is better they acknowledge that their "names are written in heaven." The presence of God can fill one with energy, but God is hidden from people who are too full of confidence in their own energy and creativity. Divinity is revealed instead to young children by intuition or to childlike (not childish) adults.

This completes the interpretation of the eight core gospel texts about Jesus and the children. We turn now to the delicate task of translating the themes found by interpreting the narratives and sayings of Jesus with a high view of children into concepts. We will then cluster the eight concepts around three propositional statements.

FROM INTERPRETATIVE THEMES TO PROPOSITIONS

My conceptual summary of the eight themes interpreted above is as follows:
1. As with the children in the market place, sometimes a game shouldn't happen —because it is the wrong game to be played.
2. A silent child is placed among the noisy disciples for ontological appreciation: it is the silent child who teaches.
3. Don't hinder children. Let them come to Jesus for a blessing, which, without speaking, they know that they need.

4. Causing children to stumble—to not be blessed?—is a matter of life and death.

5. To enter the Kingdom one needs to become like a child.

6. Nicodemus discovers the need for a complete transformation, a second naivete, to enter the Kingdom as an adult.

7. Children can intuit Jesus' presence and express their discovery.

8. Children can intuit Jesus' power in a way overconfident adults cannot.

I assert that we can further develop a theology of childhood from the above concepts by noticing children around us and remembering our own childhood. When we do this, the themes fall into three groups, each group becoming the basis of a single proposition. We will now look briefly at each proposition to gain an overview before enlarging on each of them in the next section.

FIRST PROPOSITION: HIDE-AND-SEEK

The first proposition is that our relationship with God is one of Peekaboo and, as it develops, one of Hide-and-Seek. This can be dignified in Latin by the phrase that God is *Deus Absconditus atque Praesens*. (God is hidden yet also present.) This is because we do not play Hide-and-Seek with people we know are not there. The possibility of a presence that *can* be revealed is necessary for the game to go forward.

The specific themes identified with this proposition are numbers one and six. Children will play what and with whom they please. You can't make children (or adults) play. If adults really want to know children, they need to be born again into a second naivete. This is like being born of heaven rather than earth, because it is so different from "normal" adult consciousness. These texts imply that theological Hide-and-Seek continues for a lifetime. In fact, the goal of the game *is* to keep the game going rather than end it by winning or losing.

SECOND PROPOSITION: THE SILENT CHILD

The second proposition is that it is the silent child who teaches, so adults learn from children not from what they *say*, but from how they *are*. What adults need from children is the renewal of their nonverbal powers of communication. Since human spirituality is, I would like to suggest, one of our nonverbal powers of communication, the ontological appreciation of a child is deeply important for the development of adult spirituality, which in turn supports the child's spirituality.

The themes from which we construct this proposition are two, five, seven and eight. A child teaches by being a child. To enter the Kingdom we need to become like a child. Children can intuit divinity, as the children did in the Temple when Jesus passed by. This is their nonverbal spirituality connecting with the nonverbal spirituality of Jesus. Finally, children are more open to spirituality than adults, who rely more on their abilities with words than the nonverbal communication they had before they had language.

THIRD PROPOSITION: AN ETHIC OF BLESSING

The third proposition is that blessing is a matter of life and death. Human children will not survive without a long period of nourishing relationships. The kind of relationship is as important as the fact of relationship. Jesus has shown us the quality needed for such relationships. It has the property of blessing. A blessing affirms a person and yet calls forth the best in him or her.

The themes that are gathered to make this proposition are three and four. Jesus is indignant when the disciples prevent the children from coming to him for a blessing. This is violent language, but even more violent is the language of the millstone statements. If we cause a little one to stumble (not be blessed) it is better that we be killed in an awful way. Such language suggests (to say the least) that Jesus considers the matter of blessing and not causing the little ones to stumble a matter of life and death.

We conclude, then, that the three main propositions of a theology of childhood are:
- God's elusive presence in our journey of life and death
- nonverbal communication's importance for knowing God in this journey
- an ethic of blessing to guide our actions and development on this journey

A THEOLOGY OF CHILDHOOD AND GODLY PLAY

You can see, now, how this theology guides Godly Play:
- The lessons are presented in a way that allows children to discover the hide-and-seek presence of God, community and personal meaning.
- The unspoken lesson shows what we cannot say about God's presence.
- The quality of relationships in a Godly Play environment bears the property of blessing, affirming and yet calling forth the best in the children and their adult guides.

Furthermore, getting to know children is guided by the same three propositions, which in turn guide how children disclose our maturity to us. Seeking and finding the elusive presence of children is a metaphor for God's elusive presence. Children do not reveal themselves on our timetable or by our standards of language. To know a child is a subtle art. It takes a continuing game of Hide-and-Seek. The so-called "quality time" many hope and plan for with children cannot be scheduled with any guarantee that the children will be ready when the adult is. God's disclosure works the same way. We can't trick or coerce God—or our own maturity.

DEVELOPING THE THREE MAJOR PROPOSITIONS OF A THEOLOGY OF CHILDHOOD

PROPOSITION ONE: PEEKABOO AND THE DEUS ABSCONDITUS ATQUE PRAESENS

When an infant grows restless and directs his or her sucking towards anything or anyone touched, the fundamental instinct for nourishment is enacted without which the infant will die. This activity does not so much illustrate Augustine's belief that a baby is the "most willful of all creatures" but a creature who must be in relationship to sustain life. The child is the silent bearer of this revelation.

Many mothers are so in tune with their infant's needs just after birth that the baby is not aware that there is anything "out there" or "other." Slowly an awareness of "the other" develops as the mother begins to become interested in the world around her again in addition to her focus on the newborn. Winnicott calls this "good enough mothering." It is this separation of the infant's needs and mother's needs which arouses in the infant an awareness of the other.[77]

The third step in the infant's journey is the awareness that there is a "place" between the self and the other that is not quite either and yet some of both. Winnicott called this a "transitional space" and suggested that the origins of play, religion and culture lie there. Many adults can remember their baby blanket, a stuffed animal or some other object that became for them a "transitional object," something both me and not-me.

A theological reality, it seems to me, also develops in this space. It is the fundamental game we play all our lives. It is Hide-and-Seek, which begins and continues the awareness of the Other. At first all connotations of the Other are symbolized in the mother's face, but this soon differentiates to the father or other caretakers. It continues to differentiate until we can analyze this game by means of many language games, from poetry to physics, but the theological reality never goes away.

During infancy the little ones explore what is self and what is other, as mentioned above. The theological Other of this game is there but, as yet, undifferentiated. Since there is not yet a differentiation of this ultimate search, the theological game remains unspoken as one matures.

When we play with the awareness of self and other, our theological journey is organized around what appears to be only the game of Peekaboo. Young children love to play this game, for it enlivens the relationship between the players by introducing change against a background of deep connection.

You might cover your face with your hands or some object and then uncover it to the surprise of the infant. You might drop out of sight below the edge of the crib and pop up, like a jack-in-the-box. When you utter the game's exclamation, "Peekaboo," the players laugh, unless one has been hidden too long, moved too violently or shouted too loud.

When a child begins to crawl, the game becomes Here-I-Am. When you call out, "Where are you," the little one who is hiding usually can't help but call back, "Here I am." The game is not really about hiding. It is about being found after a momentary loss of sight.

"Now *you* hide," the child laughs or gestures to the adult with his play face on.

The hiding, of course, needs to be in plain sight. Perhaps, the child will even cover you up to be sure that he or she is still in control of the hiding and being found. The certainty of the relationship is important for the game to remain in play rather than disintegrating into absolute loss and terror.

About the time children go to school and begin to interact with other children on a regular basis, the game of Hide-and-Seek becomes more complex. Now children are running and not merely crawling. They can range farther and hide better. Still, despite the emphasis on hiding or even the competition of running to a base to not be "it," the game is still one that values being found as well as hiding,

A variation of this game also develops. Sometimes a toddler will run away from mommy or daddy while laughing. When children are older and in school, they will sometimes even run away from the teacher. This is not to harass the teacher or parent but to see if the adult can be engaged in a game of Catch-Me. Children want to know if parents or teachers care enough to keep them from running clear away and disappearing.

More variations of this game appear during the teenage years. Adolescents play Hide-and-Seek with their parents and their teachers. Courtship includes many kinds of Hide-and-Seek in its rituals, even today, when custom dictates a kind of noncourtship for the development of relationships between the sexes.

Later the game of Hide-and-Seek becomes more overtly theological. Francis Thompson's poem "The Hound of Heaven" is an example. Francis Thompson (1859–1907) had not been allowed to enter the priesthood. He failed at his medical studies. Finally, he wandered the London streets, addicted to opium, but still the game with God went on, as his poem shows:

> I fled Him, down the nights and down the days;
> I fled Him, down the arches of the years;
> I fled Him, down the labyrinthine ways

Of my own mind; and in the mist of tears
I hid from Him and under running laughter.
Fear wist not to evade as Love wist to pursue.
Still with unhurrying chase,
And unperturbed pace,
Deliberate speed, majestic instancy,
Came on the following Feet,
And a Voice above their beat—
"Nought shelters thee, who wilt not shelter Me."[78]

Perhaps the poets are best at this game, but another player is Samuel Terrien, who explored this theme in biblical theology in *The Elusive Presence*.[79] His argument is that we need to trace the *experience* of God's elusive presence in the Hebrew Scriptures and the Christian Bible to discover what holds that sweeping narrative and its many genres together. One might develop a concept from this experience such as a covenant relationship, but that abstraction is based on the variety of experiences of God's elusive presence. These experiences are what the Hebrew and Christian Scriptures have in common, despite the different concepts and words by which they try to describe and explain them.

The game with the *Deus Absconditus atque Praesens* is one of being in relationship with God without being overwhelmed by God's presence or completely losing contact. This is what James P. Carse calls an "infinite game."[80] The point is for the game to continue rather than have winners and losers. Having winners and losers ends the game and, thus, disrupts the relationship. Such a relationship-breaking game is a "finite game," in Carse's terms.

The play aspect of Hide-and-Seek is not only found in the relationship with God, the Holy Trinity, but also in the serious play among the Persons of the Trinity and the play of Wisdom as mentioned in Proverbs 8:30. It is fitting that the translation of the Proverbs text shifts ambiguously between describing Wisdom as a "master workman" and a "little child." This shifting begins to sound like an event of irreducible connotation and poetry rather than a decision needing to be made between the two terms by a translator or interpreter. Maturity and childhood are always connected, as Jesus said and showed.

PROPOSITION TWO: THE SILENT CHILD TEACHES THE NECESSITY OF THE NONVERBAL

The second proposition generated by this theology of childhood is also about the importance of relationships. Children teach unconsciously all the time by their very being. The absence of language in a young child invites us to participate in nonverbal communication, although we often miss this invitation due to our frustration about teaching children how to speak like adults.

As we explored briefly in Chapter 3, Terrance Deacon's *Symbolic Species: The Co-Evolution of Language and the Brain*[81] describes the difference between non-verbal and verbal communication. Our species has developed a unique ability for language. At the same time and independently, our nonverbal communication system has developed; we share this to some extent with other creatures. It provides an interpretative frame for our verbal communication. For example, I can say exactly the same words with a smile or a sneer and mean something quite different.

In our nonverbal system we have iconic and indexical referencing. Iconic referencing is limited to signaling what is like and unlike. Indexical referencing is built up from the iconic and links connections such as smoke and fire. These two kinds of communication provide the ground from which a kind of leap takes place, a leap that produces symbolic communication. Symbols are tokens of meaning, which cannot function without social agreement. This is because they are not connected to what they refer to in any other meaningful way.

Some adults retain a special sensitivity to their iconic and indexical referencing even after symbolic-referencing is well developed. Artists who play with words, dance, stone, paint, music and other media are especially gifted at this. Children, on the other hand, have no choice but to be in tune with their iconic and indexical referencing, since their symbolic referencing is just developing. In this sense, especially, they are natural artists.

This is why Godly Play lessons are grounded in both verbal and nonverbal communication. When we speak of the importance of the "nonverbal lesson," we mean that the two systems need to be in tune for clear and direct communication. Making discords between our verbal and nonverbal communication will cause us and others to stumble. This is especially tragic for children, because it teaches discord *as* communication.

When there is discord between one's verbal and nonverbal communication, a double bind results. Children experience themselves as wrong either way they respond. Finally, the pain of discord overwhelms the need for relationship and they withdraw. Their souls wither and die.

Such discord is also tragic for adults. The roots of words pull away from their ground in the nonverbal. We cannot live in a world created by words about words without becoming insane as individuals or as cultures. Our symbolic referencing needs to be grounded in the play of our nonverbal system to be creative.

A theology of childhood celebrates the nonverbal, then, and proposes that we keep the verbal and nonverbal connected congruently. Instead of being limited to the themes of classical theology, it is alert to such themes as silence, play, laughter, crying, creating, existential awareness and spirituality which are part of our nonverbal communication system.

As Deacon has argued "Language evolved in a parallel, alongside calls and gestures, and dependent on them—indeed, language and many human nonlinguistic forms of communication probably co-evolved."[82] Godly Play, therefore, moves along the edge between the verbal and nonverbal by means of narratives, liturgy, poetry, music and other "border" kinds of communication.

Classical theology has emphasized the will and the ability to reason as the most important aspects of human being and knowing. It has also spoken of the mystery of grace and the ineffability of experiencing God. The relationship between grace and the use of our reason and will has long been studied. Perhaps a better understanding of our verbal and nonverbal communication systems, of the relationship between the limbic system and decision-making, and of the function of the two hemispheres of our brain, will help us further understand this difference between classical theology and a theology of childhood.

PROPOSITION THREE: THE NECESSITY OF RELATIONSHIPS AND THE ETHIC OF BLESSING

Finally, we come to the third proposition generated by Jesus' unique view of children: how the quality of relationships is a matter of life and death. Why was Jesus so indignant with the disciples and violent in his communication about not hindering the children? Why is it so important to neither hold them back from blessing nor make them stumble?

It is clear that our offspring will die if they are left without nurturing relationships. Our species is more helpless and dependent for a much longer time than most other kinds of creatures. We are, therefore, created with a special need for nurture. We are created to need each other. Without love we do not thrive as infants or adults even if our basic physical needs are taken care of.

Children remind us that ontology, the nature of being, is relational. We are born into this strange world to die. The only way we can be "at home" here is by being nested in creative, loving relationships. The twigs are relationships. The circle is community. The feeling of the nest is nurture.

We are oriented in our nest by four existential compass points: being at home in our relationships with others, with our own deep self, with nature and with God. The quality of these specific relationships is critical for the success of our journey.

When we teach children to rely primarily on words, we hinder the development of a sense of grounding in relationships. If our symbolic referencing is not in harmony with our iconic or indexical referencing, we will not mean what we say or say what we mean. The result of this is that we become unreal. The major way to be retuned is by being blessed in a community of blessing. To say this in as physical a way as possible, let us, therefore, talk about tossing, holding, rocking and falling.

Sometimes when babies are held too tightly or wrapped in their blankets too snugly they struggle to be free and there are tears of desperation. Their tears and cries of distress warn us that our holding has ceased to nurture growth and has begun to confine it.

Adults too experience distress when they are bound. Our warning calls may be swallowed when we are confined or controlled too tightly. We sometimes hide such distress, because dangerous relationships are better than no relationship at all.

When we mildly jostle babies, they laugh. If our tossing goes a little beyond jostling, they may also laugh, but when we toss them too high or they fall too far, there are shudders, cries and tears of fear.

If we were strong enough, and some adults are, adults too can be tossed and distressed in the same way. When this happens, we too will cry out in fear. We also cry out when we are psychologically stressed. At one end of the spectrum of relationships, people experience stress from being tightly controlled. At the opposite end of the spectrum, people experience stress from being ignored. The opposite of the tossing that scares us is being dropped. Such a loss of relationship is very hard to survive.

In the middle of the spectrum of relationships is a kind of touching that heals, rather than merely maintaining or even destroying life. This is the place of blessing, which Jesus' parable of action and indignation especially highlighted. This kind of touching provides safety and support. It encourages life rather than restricting or ignoring it.

To bless each other is a matter of ethics. Relating to our four cardinal reference points for life and death—nature, others, God and the deep self—is a matter of knowing how to act. Jesus' theme of blessing is ubiquitous in the Bible. God blessed the whole creation into being, and when God blessed Abraham, he become a blessing to God's people (Genesis 12:1-2).

Jesus blessed the children as they moved toward him. When the gospels refer to his touching, it usually infers healing. A blessing acknowledges the one who is blessed. It affirms them where they are. It also calls forth what is best in a person. It is a statement of hope and acknowledgement of what can be through healing.

The ethic of blessing, which is compressed into this image, is one that is not impersonal. Blessing is very personal. No analysis of decision-making principles is entailed.

There is moral significance and an unavoidability about decisions in ethics, but there is no "decisionism" implied here. The central focus of this image is relationships. What they do is not distinguished from who they are in community.

Blessing involves all three aspects of the moral event. It includes motive, act and results. You cannot subtract any one of these aspects of the moral situation and still have a blessing.

We need blessing. We need to move towards it. We need to be blessed and to bless. This is not merely because Jesus did. This kind of argument from authority might hold water in some Christian circles, but the argument here is based on what children and adults need to be fully human in terms of their theological definition as creatures who create in the image of the Creator. In addition, adults need to bless to awaken the child within and experience a second naivete, which in turn stimulates the children they come into contact with, which in turn stimulates adults. The generations need mutual blessings by each other to be truly Christian in the tradition of the Old and New Testaments.

This mutual blessing creates a "place" between being confined and being dropped, a place between rigidity and chaos, a place of rich complexity, which is our "home." It is a place of creativity and play. It is the wellspring of grace, a way to move forward fluidly without stumbling.

In the Sermon on the Mount (Matthew 5–7), Jesus returns to the theme of blessing and specifies the kinds of action that are blessed and bless. The poor in spirit, those who mourn, the meek, those who desire what is fair, the merciful, the pure in heart, the peacemakers, those persecuted for righteousness' sake, and those who are spoken of falsely as a way to attack Jesus—these qualities all sound like the situation society has forced children into in every century. There is power in recognizing such child-likeness. It gives us the foundation from which to call forth what is best in us.

For example, in Norwich, England, The Reverend Dr. Samuel Wells, an expert on the ethics of Stanley Hauerwas, found that the Anglican parish of St. Elizabeth's, of which he is the vicar, needed a new approach to its relationships with the community. Wells was struck by the importance of conceiving of the Church as a child rather than as a parent.

When a new building was built in 1991, there was terrible vandalism for the first five years. In conversation with a girl who had thrown rocks at the previous vicar's house, he learned that the rocks were thrown because she didn't believe in God. It was in this conversation that he discovered something about the ethic of the child and blessing, which was what the girl was really talking about.

Gradually the Church has come to see that the young person who threw the stone is in fact more representative of a widespread view, and thus more like a parent, whereas the Church, being small and not taken seriously, is in fact more like a child. The power of the Church is not that of a parent—greater resources, more experience greater physical strength; instead, the Church's power is that of the child—stubbornness and doggedness, and the tendency to ask awkward or embarrassing questions.[83]

So when the time comes to sit down with the other groups in the community, the Church sits down as a child, still learning, potentially disruptive, rather than as a parent, saying "come to where we already are." Openness to being blessed is as important as blessing.

CONCLUSION

The mutual blessing of the different ages by each other is critical for our development as human beings. Erik Erikson's stage of Generativity versus Stagnation is the longest and occurs in adulthood.[84]

Learning and cultural transmission play an enormous part in the sustaining of our species. Generativity has to do with establishing and guiding the next generation, whether it is our own children, business colleagues or personal projects. Self-absorbed individuals do not expand their interests in this way, and their investment of energy is only on themselves. This impoverishes them, and they begin to feel a sense of stagnation, thus never developing the ability to care. Such adults can take the whole human race down with them if they are powerful enough.

The failure to develop the ability to care weakens the ability to negotiate the next stage where, in Erikson's terms, the gate is Integrity versus Despair. When integrity outweighs despair, the strength of wisdom emerges. A new, timeless and accepting love is felt toward one's parents and the other significant persons in one's life. There is even a sense of comradeship with people of distant times and other callings who have left a heritage of human dignity and love.

Without wise elders we have only "elderlies" isolated in a playless old age. They are biologically sustainable but lack the wisdom to contribute to the life cycle of others or themselves. Without elders to impart wisdom, we are less sustainable as a species.

It is wisdom that brings a sense of humor to life and death, a sense of grace, which is largely unspoken. Without a sense of humor and grace the human race is especially dangerous to life in the universe. We are the only creatures powerful and creative enough to cope with the most dangerous life form of all—*ourselves*. Is it then too apocalyptic to say that Godly Play—in whatever form you choose to engage with it, by whatever name you choose to call it—is a matter of life and death?

REFLECTING: A THEOLOGY OF CHILDHOOD

- What practices reflect a low view of childhood in your community? Your church? Your ministry?

....

....

....

....

....

- What practices reflect a high view of childhood in your community? Your church? Your ministry?

....

....

....

....

....

- Choose one of the eight stories of Jesus about childhood (pp. 122-130). What about this story do you like best?

....

....

....

....

....

- What part of this story is the most important part?

....

....

....

....

....

- Where are you in this story or what part of this story is about you?

....

....

....

....

....

- Where in your life can you identify the experience of playing Hide-and-Seek with God? Where in your life would you like to make more room for this experience?

....

....

....

....

....

- Where in your life can you identify the experience of holy silence? Where in your life would you like to make more room for this experience?

....

....

....

....

....

- Where in your life can you identify the experience of living out the ethic of blessing? Where in your life would you like to make more room for this experience?

....

....

....

....

....

EPILOGUE

A LAST STORY

UNSTABLE NATIVITY

The church stood on a high promontory. Its spire pointed beyond the vanishing point. Inside a game of Hide-and-Seek was played each week. Sometimes God hid. Sometimes the people did. Everyone won when the bread and wine were shared, tasting of time and space.

One day a priest walked carefully through the nave inspecting the sacred precincts. He then moved on to the narthex and, finally stood before an oak door. The great key was turned with some difficulty in the lock, then the door was gradually pulled open.

Down he went around the circular, stone staircase into the deepest part of the structure below the great tower. At the bottom was a round room. A carved, wooden chair sat at its center. It seemed rooted there. The priest did not sit. It was not for sitting. No one could remember what it was for.

As he looked around the room, the priest slowly sensed something was amiss. Then he saw it! A tiny, almost transparent plant was pushing its tendrils up underneath the chair from between two stones.

He lunged and tried to yank it out by the roots, but it would not budge. Next, he tried to snap it off like glass, but it bent like soft plastic. Finally, he got down on his knees. He did not pray but cut the plant off cleanly with a sharp knife. All was immaculate again, but the priest was sweating as he started back up the stairs.

A few days went by, but the growth kept coming to mind. The priest went back to see if all was well. It was not.

The plant had grown once more above the level of the floor. It was cut down again and again. Soon, everyone knew it was true. When you trimmed the growth it grew stronger.

A special council decided that the intrusion must be buried beneath a new floor, laid over the old one. Stonemasons were summoned, and the work was done.

The next week the inspecting priest unlocked the oak door and descended the stone stairs. He struggled back up the steps in shock to shout for help. When everyone gathered in the circular room, each carried a lantern. Hundreds of slender, transparent runners glistened along the walls and ceiling in the flickering light. As they watched, rocks came loose and clattered to the floor. It was worse than anyone could imagine. The growth was escaping!

The priests became frantic. Workmen were called that very night. They carried stones into the church by torchlight and rolled them down into the depths. Soon the whole room was filled with rocks and cement. Finally, during the dark days of winter, the doorway was sealed. By the time the snow slid with a crash from the green copper roof in spring, the victory seemed won.

The people of the village had not been told about the struggle, but they had seen it. What was all that rock for? they wondered. As the weather warmed, their minds turned to other things, especially after a particular midweek service.

The liturgy at midweek was quiet, since only a few people came to pray. You could almost hear the sunlight sliding through the glass and bursting into colors.

One day, the faint sound of weeping was heard, but no one crying could be found. A few weeks later, traces of moisture began to shine on the great front window. No natural explanation could be found.

The sound of weeping grew stronger as the summer months past. By fall moisture ran like tears down the front window. Once a priest put his finger into the water and tasted it, as a joke, to see if it was salty. It was.

Now many strangers came to the church. They listened with the parish for the weeping and watched the water run down the glass. In their devotion they missed the small cracks that appeared in the walls. When the great beams above them groaned, they were startled and looked up, but the vaulted ceiling was too high for them to see how strained the timbers were.

During late autumn a fine dust settled over everything in the church. No matter how much cleaning was done, more was always needed. The dust sifted into the holy bread and wine and into the stiff collars of the priests. Everyone was uncomfortable, but the people did not stop coming until their itching turned to fear.

By winter the wood shrieked. The building shuddered. No songs were sung nor services said. Nothing could be heard inside but the splintering wood, the creaking roof and the falling stones.

On Christmas morning the clergy tried to celebrate the birth of Christ in that place. When they entered the dangerous church they were stunned. In the night the roof had split open! Bits of slate and copper still banged and clattered against the stone floor and broken oak pews. Above them was the winter sky.

As they tried to take this in, huge pieces of wood, chunks of rock, fragments of plaster and even bells began to fall like an avalanche inside the great spire. The whole structure was about to break up! The priests ran out into the snow, their robes flying behind them.

As far away as the priests could run, they stood, panting and gasping for breath in the cold. You could see their breath circling them as they turned fearfully around to see the church again. What they saw was that the great tower had let itself down with immense dignity. It did not topple over. It came down inside itself, catching its own rubble as it fell.

Choked with dust and ruin, the priests, shivering in the cold, wiped tears from their eyes. The earth shuddered under them, and their ears throbbed with blood when the sound of the catastrophe reached them. They could barely stand as the thick cloud of destruction enveloped them and blotted out the holy place they had grown to know so well.

A breeze came up and the cloud began to thin. What they saw when it disappeared sent them to their knees, making the sign of the cross.

Some said they saw an almost transparent tree, rising as tall as the old tower. Others only shook their heads and said nothing. Most saw a broken shell, shattered beyond repair. They went away grim and cynical and sad.

More snow came. The ruin lay alone all winter. No one had the courage to even think about it. There was too much brokenness to risk caring about.

In the spring people began to go near the place again. Tiny chimes seemed to ring among the sparkling leaves above, and laughter was heard below where the tree's shadow fell. Children wandered in the ruins with wide eyes, picking up chunks of colored glass, slate, copper, stone, wood, brass and the scattered pages of cracked books to play with. They held these fragments up to the light and put them together in new ways. The desolation became a playground, and the birds of the air came and made their nests there.

One day a child pressed a piece of colored glass against the tree, which all of the children could easily see. The glass stuck. It could not be pulled away. People tried to dislodge it, because it was so beautiful, reflecting light's spectrum like a prism. As the old church's pieces became embedded in the living presence of the tree, it became visible to everyone.

Outsiders watched with disbelief. "This could not happen," they said. "Physics and politics do not allow such things." Delight ascended despite all natural and social law.

Slowly, over the years, the pieces of the old church grew together into a mixture of old and new, until it was done again. It was wide as well as tall, and finally a door opened, seemingly by itself. People went inside and rested in the shade. The wind, leaves and birds sang with the organ pipes to join the violins and voices singing. It was too good and beautiful to be true, yet there it was.

Years went by. The new church became old. The flickering but steady state, like candle flame, dimmed to the stable state of crystal. The liturgical year began to turn like a windup toy, ornamenting the repression of its depth.

One day a new young priest took a key from her ring and unlocked the ponderous door. Down she went around the winding stairs into the depths of the church. There she found something growing between the stones under the chair. The stable place had become unstable once again. Nativity was breaking out!

And it still does...

MORE INFORMATION ON GODLY PLAY

The Complete Guide to Godly Play, Volumes 1-4 by Jerome Berryman, is available from Living the Good News (Denver, 2002). *Volume 1: How To Lead Godly Play Lessons* is the essential handbook for using Godly Play in church school or a wide variety of alternative settings. *Volumes 2-4* present complete Session plans for Fall, Winter and Spring.

The *Center for the Theology of Childhood* is the organization that sponsors ongoing research, training, accreditation programs, the development of a theology of childhood for adults and support of Godly Play. The Center maintains a schedule of training and speaking events related to Godly Play, as well as a list of trainers available throughout this and other countries for help in establishing Godly Play programs. *Contact information:*

> Center for the Theology of Childhood at Christ Church Cathedral
> 1117 Texas Avenue
> Houston, TX 77002
> (713) 223-4305
> fax: (713) 223-1041
> e-mail: theologychild2@earthlink.net
> www.godlyplay.net and www.godlyplay.org (a discussion group)

Godly Play Resources crafts beautiful and lasting materials suitable for use in a Godly Play classroom. Although you can make your own materials, many teachers find their work both simplified and enriched by using Godly Play Resources to supply their classrooms. *Contact information:*

> Godly Play Resources
> P.O. Box 563
> Ashland KS 67831
> (800) 445-4390
> fax: (620) 635-2191
> *www.godlyplay.com*

Dallas Children's Medical Center includes the Godly Play approach in their program for pastoral care. This is an accredited center for Clinical Pastoral Education and for teaching the speciality of pediatric pastoral care. *Contact information:*

> The Reverend Ron Somers-Clark
> Chaplain and Director of Pastoral Care
> Children's Medical Center of Dallas
> 1935 Motor Street
> Dallas TX 75235-7794
> (214) 640-2822

ENDNOTES

[1] Catherine Garvey, *Play* (Cambridge, Mass: Harvard University Press,1977).

[2] Jean LeClerq, *The Love of Learning and the Desire for God: A Study of Monastic Culture* (New York: Fordham University Press, 1982).

[3] Emily Dickinson, *Dickenson*, selected by Peter Washington (New York: Knopf, 1993), 30.

[4] Stuart Brown, "Introduction," *ReVision*, 17, no. 4 (Spring, 1995), 2.

[5] Ibid., "Evolution and Play," 9.

[6] Brian Sutton-Smith, *The Ambiguity of Play* (Cambridge, Mass: Harvard University Press, 1977), 7-8.

[7] Ibid., 8.

[8] Ibid., 214.

[9] Garvey, *Play*, 4-5.

[10] Howard Gardner, *The Arts and Human Development* (New York: Basic Books, 1994).

[11] David Miller, *Gods and Games: Toward a Theology of Play* (New York: Harper and Row, Colophon Books, 1973).

[12] Jurgen Moltmann, *Theology of Play* (New York: Harper and Row, 1972).

[13] Ibid., 111-113.

[14] Johan Huizerga, *Homo Ludens* (Boston: Beacon Press, 1955).

[15] William Golding, *Lord of the Flies* (Berkeley: Perigree Books, 1954), 12.

[16] Ibid., 21.

[17] Ibid., 127.

[18] Ibid., 137.

[19] Ibid., 139.

[20] Tom Shippey, *J. R .R. Tolkien: Author of the Century* (New York: Houghton Mifflin, 2001).

[21] Ibid., 130-135.

[22] Eric Berne, *Games People Play* (New York: Grove Press, 1964).

[23] Ibid., 176.

[24] Frederick Buechner, *Wishful Thinking: A Seeker's ABC, Revised and Expanded* (San Francisco: HarperSanFrancisco, 1993), 38.

[25] Ibid, 33.

[26] Ibid, 34.

[27] Robert Farrar Capon, *Between Noon and Three* (Grand Rapids, Mich.: Wm. B. Eerdmans, 1997), 96.

[28] Ibid., 113.

[29] Beuchner, *Wishful Thinking,* 49.

[30] Mihaly Csikszentmihalyi, *Flow: The Psychology of Optimal Experience* (New York: HarperCollins, 1990).

[31] Examples are Rheta De Vries and Lawrence Kohlberg, *Programs in Early Education: The Constructivist View* (New York: Longman, 1987). Further discussion of this may be found in John Chattin-McNichols, *The Montessori Controversy* (Albany, NY: Delmar Publishers, 1992).

[32] David Elkind, "Piaget and Montessori," *Harvard Educational Review* (Fall, 1967).

[33] Rita Kramer, *Maria Montessori* (New York: G. P. Putnam's Sons, 1976), 251.

[34] E. M. Standing Archives. Notes taken by Standing. Apparently, Ted Standing was not famous for his Italian. Cavalletti mentioned this to me November 21, 1991, in Rome and said that she had never heard of such a construction in Italian. Standing may have misheard or misspelled some combination of the verbs *alzarsi* (to rise up) and *balzare* (to leap).

[35] E. M. Standing, ed., *The Child in the Church* (St. Paul, Minn.: Catechetical Guild, 1965), 23.

[36] Maria Montessori, *The Absorbent Mind* (New York: Dell Publishing Co., 1967), 176-177. An earlier and more complete statement of her views on the imagination may be found in *Spontaneous Activity in Education: The Advanced Montessori Method* (New York: Schocken Books, 1965.

[37] Ibid, 177.

[38] Montessori, *To Educate the Human Potential* (Thiruvanmiyur, Madras, India: Kalakshetra Publications, 1948).

[39] Montessori, *The Absorbent Mind*, 290.

[40] E. M. Standing, *Maria Montessori: Her Life and Work* (New York: Penguin, 1984).

[41] Ibid., "Author's Note."

[42] Massimo Grazzini, *Bibliografia Montessori* (Brescia, Italy: La Scuola Editrice, 1965).

[43] Standing, *Maria Montessori*, 69.

[44] Kramer, *Maria Montessori*, 275.

[45] Standing, *The Child in the Church* (1965), 77.

[46] Ibid., 80.

[47] E. M. Standing, ed., *The Child in the Church* (London and Edinburgh: Sands and Co., 1929), 52.

[48] Standing, *The Child in the Church* (1965), 132.

[49] E. M. Standing Archives.

[50] E. M. Standing, *The Montessori Revolution in Education* (New York: Schocken Books, 1962).

[51] Standing, *The Child in the Church* (1965), 131.

[52] Sofia Cavalletti, "L'itinerario spirituale di Eugenio Zolli" *Responsibilita del Sapere* (April–September, 1956), 221-252.

[53] Sofia Cavalletti, *The Religious Potential of the Child: The Description of an Experience with Children from Ages Three to Six* (Ramsey/New York: Paulist Press, 1983), 161. *Il Potenziale religioso del bambino* (Rome: Citta Nuova Editrice, 1979).

[54] Ibid., 164.

[55] Standing, *The Child in the Church* (1965), 215-216.

[56] Josef A. Jungmann, *Die Frohbotschaft und unsere Glaubensverkundigung* (withdrawn from publication, 1936). *The Good News Yesterday and Today*, ed. Johannes Hofinger, trans., abridged, and noted by William A. Huesman (New York: W. H. Sadlier, 1962). This was the 25th anniversary of *Die Frohbotshaft*.

[57] Mary C. Boys, Biblical Interpretation in Religious Education: A Study of the *Kerygmatic Era* (Birmingham, Alabama: Religious Education Press, 1980), 81-82. This book is a most helpful source for the background and an interpretation of the rise and fall of salvation history in the religious education of North America.

[58] Josef A. Jungmann, *Glaubensverkundigung im Lichte der Frohbotschaft* (Insbruck, Vienna, Munich, Tyrolia Verlag, 1963). *Announcing the Word of God*, trans. Ronald Walls (New York: Herder and Herder, 1967).

[59] Sofia Cavalletti, "Il liturgismo del metodo Montessori" (Liturgy and the Montessori Method) *L'Osservatore Romano* (Vatican City, 19 December 1962).

60 Cavalletti, *The Religious Potential of the Child*, 45.

61 Henry Chadwick, *Augustine* (Oxford: Oxford University Press, 1986), 2.

62 Augustine, translated by Henry Chadwick, *Confessions* (Oxford: Oxford University Press, 1991), 9.

63 Marcia J. Bunge, *The Child in Christian Thought* (Grand Rapids, Mich.: Wm. B. Eerdmans, 2001), 350.

64 Karl Rahner, *Theological Investigations,* vol. 8 (London: Darton, Longman and Todd, 1971), 33-50.

65 Mary Ann Hinsdale, "Infinite Openness to the Infinite: Karl Rahner's Contribution to Modern Catholic Thought on the Child" in Marcia J. Bunge (ed.), *The Child in Christian Thought* (Grand Rapids, Mich.: Wm. B. Eerdmans, 2000), 406-445.

66 John N. Kohlenberger, III. *The NRSV Concordance Unabridged* (Grand Rapids, Mich.: The Zondervan Corporation, 1991).

67 Hans-Ruedi Weber, *Jesus and the Children* (Loveland, Ohio: Treehaus Communications, 1994).

68 Bunge, *The Child in Christian Thought*, 29-60.

69 Weber, *Jesus and the Children*, 2.

70 Ibid., 7, 21.

71 Ibid., 7.

72 Ibid., 6.

73 Ibid., 11.

74 Diane J. Hymans, *The Role of Play in a Cultural-Linguistic Approach to Religion: Theoretical Implications for Education in the Faith Community* (D. Ed. Dissertation, The Presbyterian School of Christian Education, Richmond, Virginia, 1992).

75 Weber, *Jesus and the Children*, 19.

76 James W. Fowler, *Stages of Faith: The Psychology of Human Development and the Quest for Meaning* (San Francisco: Harper and Row, 1981).

77 D. Winnicott, *Playing and Reality* (New York:Basic Books, 1971).

78 M. H. Abrams, General Editor, *The Norton Anthology of English Literature, Volume 2* (New York: W. W. Norton & Company, 1962), 1053.

79 Samuel Terrien, *The Elusive Presence: The Heart of Biblical Theology* (New York: HarperCollins, 1983).

80 James P. Carse, *Finite and Infinite Games: A Vision of Life* (New York: Ballantine, 1987).

81 Terrence Deacon, *The Symbolic Species: The Co-Evolution of Language and the Brain* (New York: W. W. Norton, 1997).

82 Deacon, *The Symbolic Species*, 540.

83 Mark Thiessen Nation and Samuel Wells, *Faithfulness and Fortitude: In Conversation with the Theological Ethics of Stanley Hauerwas* (Edinburgh: T&T Clark, 2000), 123.

84 Erik Erikson, *Childhood and Society, 2nd ed.* (New York: W. W. Norton, 1963).

BIBLIOGRAPHY

Berne, Eric. *Games People Play*. New York: Grove Press, 1964.

Boys, Mary C. *Biblical Interpretation in Religious Education: A Study of the Kerygmatic Era*. Birmingham, Alabama: Religious Education Press, 1980.

Brown, Stuart. *Revision*, vol. 17, no. 4 (Spring, 1993). In addition to Brown's "Introduction" and "Evolution and Play," the entire issue is relevant.

Bunge, Marcia J. *The Child in Christian Thought*. Grand Rapids, Michigan: Wm. B. Eerdmans, 2001.

Cavalletti, Sofia. "L'itinerario spirituale di Eugenio Zolli," *Responsibilita del Sapere*. April–September, 1956.

_____. *The Religious Potential of the Child: The Description of an Experience with Children from Ages Three to Six*. Ramsey/New York: Paulist Press, 1983; *Il Potenziale religioso del bambino* Rome: Citta Nuova Editrice, 1979.

_____. "Il liturgismo del metodo Montessori" *L'Osservatore Romano*. Vatican City, 19 December 1962.

Chadwick, Henry. *Augustine*. Oxford: Oxford University Press, 1986.

_____. *Confessions.* Oxford: Oxford University Press, 1991.

Chattin-McNichols, John. *The Montessori Controversy.* Albany, NY: Delmar Publishers, 1992.

Deacon, Terrence. *The Symbolic Species: The Co-Evolution of Language and the Brain*. New York: W. W. Norton, 1997.

De Vries, Rheta and Lawrence Kohlberg. *Programs in Early Education: The Constructivist View*. New York: Longman, 1987.

Elkind, David. "Piaget and Montessori," *Harvard Educational Review*. Fall, 1967.

Erikson, Erik. *Childhood and Society, 2nd ed.* New York: W. W. Norton, 1963.

Fowler, James W. *Stages of Faith: The Psychology of Human Development and the Quest for Meaning*. San Francisco: Harper and Row, 1981.

Gardner, Howard. *The Arts and Human Development*. New York: Basic Books, 1994.

_____. *Creating Minds*. New York: Basic Books, 1993

Garvey, C. *Play*. Cambridge, Mass.: Harvard University Press, 1974.

Golding, William. *Lord of the Flies*. Perigee Books, Berkley Publishing, 1959.

Grazzini, Massimo. *Bibliografia Montessori*. Brescia, Italy: La Scuola Editrice, 1965.

Huizinga, Johan. *Homo Ludens*. Boston: Beacon Press, 1955.

Hymans, Diane J. *The Role of Play in a Cultural-Linguistic Approach to Religion: Theoretical Implications for Education in the Faith Community*. D. Ed. Dissertation, The Presbyterian School of Christian Education, Richmond, Virginia, 1992.

Jungmann, Josef A. *Die Frohbotschaft und unsere Glaubensverkundigung* (withdrawn from publication, 1936). *The Good News Yesterday and Today*, ed. Johannes Hofinger, trans., abridged, and noted by William A. Huesman. New York: W. H. Sadlier, 1962.

Jungmann, Josef A. *Glaubensverkundigung im Lichte der Frohbotschaft*. Insbruck, Vienna, Munich, Tyrolia Verlag, 1963; *Announcing the Word of God*, trans. Ronald Walls. New York: Herder and Herder, 1967.

Kohlenberger, III, John N. *The NRSV Concordance Unabridged*. Grand Rapids, Mich.: The Zondervan Corporation, 1991.

Kramer, Rita. *Maria Montessori*. New York: G. P. Putnam's Sons, 1976.

LeClerq, Jean. *The Love of Learning and the Desire for God: A Study of Monastic Culture*. New York: New American Library, 1962.

Miller, David. *Gods and Games: Toward a Theology of Play*. New York: Harper and Row, Colophon Books, 1973.

Montessori, Maria. *The Absorbent Mind*. New York: Dell Publishing Co., 1967.

_____. *To Educate the Human Potential*. Madras, India: Kalakshetra Publications, 1948.

Moltmann, Jurgen. *Theology of Play*. New York: Harper and Row, 1972.

Nation, Mark Thiessen and Samuel Wells. *Faithfulness and Fortitude: In Conversation with the Theological Ethics of Stanley Hauerwas*. Edinburgh: T&T Clark, 2000.

Rahner, Karl. *Theological Investigations*. London: Darton, Longman and Todd, 1971.

Standing, E. M., ed. *The Child in the Church*. London and Edinburgh: Sands and Co., 1929; St. Paul, Minn.: Catechetical Guild, 1965.

_____. *Maria Montessori: Her Life and Works.* London: Hollis and Carter Ltd., 1957; New York: New American Library, 1984.

_____. *The Montessori Revolution in Education*. New York: Schocken Books, 1962.

Sutton-Smith, Brian. *The Ambiguity of Play*. Cambridge, Mass.: Harvard University Press, 1997.

Terrien, Samuel. *The Elusive Presence: The Heart of Biblical Theology*. New York: HarperCollins, 1983

Weber, Hans-Ruedi. *Jesus and the Children*. Loveland, Ohio: Treehaus Communications, 1994.

Winnicott, D. *Playing and Reality*. New York: Basic Books, 1971.